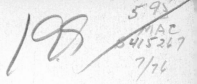

Canadian Forestry

The View Beyond the Trees

by
Chas. R. Stanton

Contents

Macmillan of Canada
Maclean-Hunter Press

Cette publication est disponible en français sous le titre
La foresterie au Canada — Au delà des arbres.

To Have . . . and To Use

Great changes have been wrought in the concept of forestry in Canada. No longer does the term simply conjure up images of felling and hauling great timbers from the forest. We have come to learn that the forest holds many values for all of us besides those of wood and fibre. We are aware of its role in regulating the quantity and quality of our water supplies. We perceive it as a home for wildlife which we may hunt or quietly observe. We are increasingly aware of its recreational worth for people contending with the exacting demands of a rapidly changing world. With all this, we are also becoming more conscious of some of the complex ecological and social problems that must be faced.

The interaction of one use of the forest upon another requires our intimate understanding lest we jeopardize the quality or quantity of those values which we seek. Francis Bacon summed it up succinctly when he stated that, "Nature, to be commanded, must be obeyed."

As greater pressures are exerted on the forest, the demands of individual groups of people can no longer be assessed in isolation. Due consideration must be accorded to other sections of society and, indeed, to the people of the country as a whole.

Ecologists, environmentalists, and others tell us how cautious and well-founded must be the management of our forests if their numerous benefits are to be ours in perpetuity. The provision of such management is the challenge of forestry in Canada today.

1
Captain James Cook visits the Nootka
Indians on the west coast of Vancouver
Island in 1778. Wooden native houses
are portrayed in the background.

Settlement, War, and the Forest

Canada's Indian peoples, relatively few
in numbers and reliant at the outset on
stone-age tools, can hardly be said to
have practised forestry. Nevertheless,
trees and shrubs provided them with
materials for shelter and transportation
as well as items of food.

Many of the west coast Indian tribes
constructed impressive wooden houses
framed with heavy pole timbers and
sheathed with straight-grained western
red cedar. These were long-term dwellings. The more nomadic tribes to the
east of the Rocky Mountains did not build
such solid shelters, but they still relied
on trees for poles and bark which, along
with skins, were used extensively in
constructing their less permanent tepees
and lodges.

The Indians also relied on the forest
for canoe materials. On the west coast
dugouts were favoured. In this region,
river canoes were constructed from cot-

tonwood logs while seagoing vessels were made from the more buoyant cedar. However, with the exception of the west coast tribes, most of Canada's Indians preferred bark-covered canoes. Though frail, such craft were light and easily portaged. If damaged, repairs were easily effected. The canoeist simply stitched on new strips of bark with threads of spruce root and sealed the seams with spruce gum. Birch bark was the commonest covering and also the most satisfactory.

The forests were also important to the Indians as a source of food. For the west coast tribes there were elderberries, crab-apples, huckleberries and many other fruits and roots, some of which were gathered and stored for winter use. The Plains Indians had wild cherries and serviceberries while further to the east the Iroquoian tribes used hickory nuts, chestnuts, butternuts, and acorns.

In the east, too, many tribes collected the maple sap for its sugar. The sugar maple tree was slashed with a tomahawk and a wooden chip or spout inserted to direct the fluid, drop by drop, into a birch-bark container. The sap was reduced by boiling in earthenware pots if such were available. Alternatively, a hollowed-out log was often used as a receptacle and by repeatedly dropping hot rocks into this sap trough the sugar was eventually recovered.

The foregoing provides a glimpse of some of the direct benefits the Indians gained from trees and shrubs. But, of course, the forest had even more to offer. It was a home for a rich variety of wildlife. Beaver, deer, elk, bear and many other species were hunted for their meat or pelts. Forest streams and lakes yielded fish. Food and clothing from the wildlife of the forest domain contributed greatly to the Indians' way of life, and indeed, their survival.

The Indians drew on the bounty of the forest as they required. They were sustained by it and the forest itself continued essentially undiminished. This, then, was the situation that prevailed when the first explorers and settlers arrived from Europe.

In 1608, Samuel de Champlain, acting on behalf of the Company of One Hundred Associates, built a fort at the base of Quebec cliffs and initiated the first European settlement of Canada. From then until the Treaty of Paris in 1763, when New France was ceded to Great Britain, only faltering steps were taken towards reaping the forest harvest and setting up the forest products trade for which Canada was to become noted in later centuries.

2
The Haida Indians of the Queen Charlotte Islands, displaying considerable carpentry skills, built substantial houses from western red cedar.

3
The forest provided all needed materials for birch-bark canoe and wigwam.

4
Canada's forests furnished masts and spars for warships from early settlement until the era of iron ships.

5
Cutting, piling, and burning was the simplest method of clearing the forest and preparing the way for agriculture.

4

The French placed reservations on oak and white pine for the use of their navy, but, in spite of these actions, many trees which would have made prime naval timbers fell prey to the local sawmills that sprang up before the end of the 17th century. Trade in ship masts was also seriously hampered by a shortage of appropriate ships to carry them back to the mother country. One record tells of a seven-year delay from the time of cutting until the arrival of the mast cargo in France.

Nevertheless, before 1700, the colony had an export trade in masts and spars with the West Indies and in later years she developed her own shipbuilding industry along the St. Lawrence River. Ten vessels, ranging in size from 40 to 100 tons (41 to 102 t),* were built in 1752. Sawmills steadily increased in numbers so that by 1734 a total of 52 were in operation east of the Ottawa River. However, in spite of these developments, lumber exports by 1759 were valued at only $31 250.

After 1763, British authorities, in turn, were quick to proclaim reservations on lands bearing timber suitable for naval purposes. This applied especially to stands of white pine which were prized for masts. Following the American Revo-

5

*An explanation of the metric symbols used is found on page (69).

lution, Great Britain lost her mast supplies from Maine and New Hampshire and consequently turned her attention more directly to Canadian sources and in particular to the mast timbers available along the Saint John and Miramichi rivers in what is now New Brunswick.

With the advent of American independence there was an influx of Loyalists into Canada from the United States. These were people who had supported George III in the revolutionary war and who now sought to make another start outside of the new republic. Land grants were made to the Loyalists with settlement concentrating in New Brunswick, Nova Scotia, the Eastern Townships of Quebec, the north shore of Lake Ontario, and down through the fertile peninsula that stretches southward between Lake Huron and Lake Erie. In these areas the newcomers were confronted by forest which rapidly fell prey to their axes as a first step in converting the land to agriculture. True, they used part of what they cut for buildings and the production of potash and charcoal, but by far the greatest portion was simply burned. And thus, much forest wealth was sacrificed to permit a needed agriculture to flourish — a situation replicated by pioneers in many parts of the world.

It now remained for the French wars, which broke out in 1793, to concentrate Great Britain's attention on the real development of the timber trade that was in time to grow and diversify into Canada's lucrative, present-day forest products industry. Before these wars, most of Great Britain's wood imports, including ship masts, came from the Baltic countries, but at the same time there was a trend towards increasing reliance on North American supplies. In 1808, however, Napoleon's Continental System came into full force shutting off all but a small trickle of supplies from the Baltic countries. This posed an immediate problem for the navy and timber merchants alike and a sudden and dramatic change in timber trade with British North America resulted. Mast imports almost quadrupled in a single year to reach a total of 16 729. In 1807, 27 000 loads* of timber were imported. In 1808, this increased to 57 000 loads and the following year the figure mounted to 90 000. Most of this was brought about by the letting of profitable contracts and the establishment of high freight rates. Later, the duty on foreign timber was doubled, further favouring development of the colonial trade.

Besides providing masts and spars for British ships, Canada's timber trade quickly expanded in the early 19th cen-

6
Squaring timber in the Ontario forest about 1900; a job for a keen eye and even keener blade

tury to meet growing British domestic requirements for square timber and deals. Square timber was made by hewing logs, usually white pine, to a square cross-section. This process, which called for considerable skill on the part of the axeman, also proved decidedly wasteful of wood. Square timbers were hauled from the bush, assembled into rafts, and floated downstream to the timber port of Quebec for loading aboard the ships bound for Great Britain. Deals were made by sawing logs into planks 3 inches (7.6 cm) or more in thickness. It took considerable capital and skill to set up and operate deal sawmills and this industry developed somewhat more slowly than did the production of square timber; nevertheless, by 1815 it was firmly established.

From 1821, the high tariffs, established during the wars with France, were successively reduced to disappear entirely in 1866. Each reduction was preceded by a rush to get timber to England before it took effect. Immediately afterwards there was a great drop in trade. These fluctuations brought ruin to many in the timber business, but, in spite of this instability, successive export peaks climbed. This situation was due to the good qualities of Canadian white pine

*The traditional measurement for square timber was the "load" of 50 cubic feet (1.4 m³).

7
Close by Canada's Parliament Buildings, a square-timber raft is readied for the long journey down the Ottawa and St. Lawrence rivers.

8
At the timber coves of Quebec, rafts were broken down and loaded aboard overseas vessels.

and also to the rapid growth of the British market which was able to absorb supplies from both the colonies and the Baltic countries.

For about the first 30 years or so of the 19th century, Canadian trade in timber was confined to the British market. Thereafter, however, a trade in sawn lumber began to develop with the United States. At the outset, this took the planks and boards from small sawmills and was diffused along the length of the border. Starting in 1848, more American capital moved into Canada along with American lumbermen who set about the business of establishing mills and machinery to produce lumber specifically for the United States market. This new trade continued to grow and by the end of the century it was about equal in value to that with Great Britain.

Around 1865, the square timber trade started to decline as a result of uncertainties of production and demand coupled with the gradual exhaustion of the best virgin pine areas of eastern Canada. Producers also found that it was more profitable to manufacture deals for the British market or boards and planks for the American trade. By the turn of the century square timbers had practically disappeared. The deal trade sur-

9
From the 1860's to 1890's oxen were used to skid logs in British Columbia forests; then horses took over because they proved to be more mobile and better pullers. In their turn, horses were replaced by steam donkey engines, one of which is seen in the background.

10
Oxen and horses were also used in eastern Canada, often drawing timber by sleigh.

11
Steam locomotives also played an important role in delivering timber to the mills.
12
Some gentlemen of stature and influence at an Ottawa Valley lumber camp
13
The Canada Paper Company's mill at Windsor Mills, Quebec, about 1910

11

12

vived only a little longer. Here too, shortage of high-grade material coupled with the attractions of the growing American market for boards and planks was mainly responsible.

While it is not known precisely when the first lumber mill was built in eastern Canada there were indications of a local trade in lumber in Quebec shortly after 1650, and before the end of the 17th century several sawmills were operating along the St. Lawrence River. In the west, British Columbia sawmills began to make their appearance on Vancouver Island about 1848. Exports of western lumber started in the 1860's and went mainly to South America, Australia, and San Francisco. However, completion of the Panama Canal in 1914 opened up European markets for the fine lumber of British Columbia.

The eastern lumber industry rapidly declined after World War I while that of British Columbia grew until it accounted for more than half of the total Canadian production. In the east, readily accessible merchantable timber had been depleted, operating costs had risen, and trade with Britain had fallen off in the face of competition from the Baltic countries. In addition, the Hawley-Smoot Tariff

13

both pulp and paper. The first few years of World War II saw great increases in pulp production although these were somewhat reduced later as more manpower and electricity were diverted to war needs. However, in the postwar era the industry continued its upward climb. In 1973, Canada had a total of 146 mills involved in pulp and/or paper manufacture. Together they shipped in excess of $3.7 billion worth of goods.

Act 1930, and the United States Revenue Act 1932, virtually closed the United States market to Canadian timber. However, from 1933 until the beginning of World War II there was a steady improvement in export markets resulting mainly from the establishment of the Imperial Preference and the signing of new trade agreements with the United States.

With the outbreak of war, Britain was once again cut off from her Baltic supplies and lumber production rose dramatically to meet British needs as well as those of the United States and Canada. In the postwar period, domestic demand for lumber continued to be extraordinarily high and exports reached unprecedented heights. Production stood at 5 billion board feet (23 million cubic metres)* in 1946 and doubled to 10 billion board feet (45 million cubic metres) by the mid-60's. In 1973 it exceeded 15 billion board feet (68 million cubic metres).

For the greater part of her forest history Canada has been concerned with extracting timber from the forest and converting it into various wood products from ship masts to sawn lumber as has been outlined. However, in the latter half of the 19th century a new and far-reach-

ing development began to take place. A growing demand for paper quickly exhausted the supply of rags from which most paper was then made and, by experimenting, paper-makers were led to the use of wood fibre as a substitute.

In 1866, at Valleyfield in Quebec, probably the first wood grinder in North America began operations, and in 1869 the first chemical wood pulp mill in Canada commenced production at Windsor Mills, near Sherbrooke, in Quebec. The 1880's saw an expansion in the use of wood pulp for paper-making in eastern Canada but it was not until 1901 that wood pulping operations began in British Columbia.

From the turn of the century until 1918, the value of pulp and paper production made a prodigious leap from something in excess of $8 million to well over $100 million. It was during these early years that the mills began specializing in newsprint for which Canada was destined to become the world's major supplier. Apart from a small drop in output in 1921 and a decline in the depression years of the early 1930's, the pulp and paper industry steadily gained ground. By 1939, there were 27 mills making pulp only, 24 manufacturing paper only, and 49 producing

*There is no true counterpart for the board foot in the metric system. However, approximate equivalents are given in cubic metres using a conversion factor of 4.53 m³ per 1000 board feet.

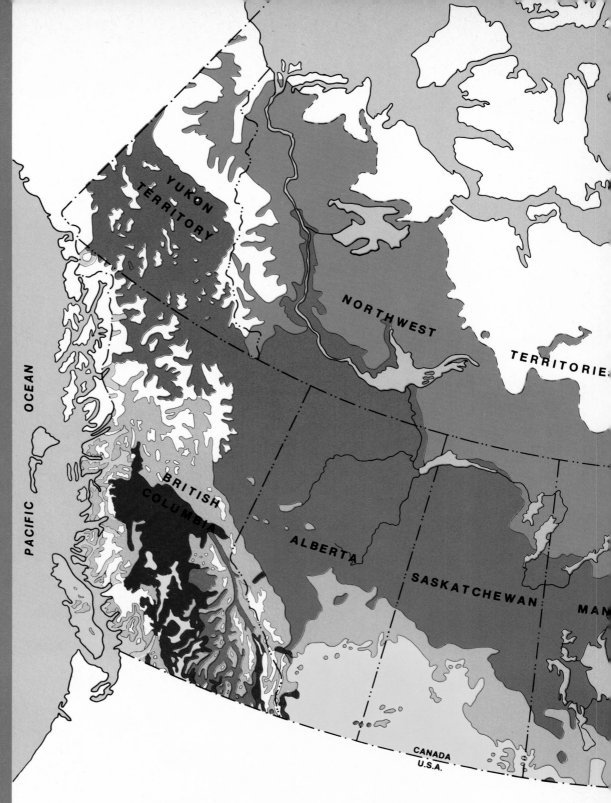

Canada's Forests Today

Forest Regions	Principal Tree Species	Forest Regions	Principal Tree Species
Boreal		Coast	Western Red Cedar, Western Hemlock, Sitka Spruce, Douglas-fir.
Predominantly Forest	White and Black Spruce, Balsam Fir, Jack Pine, White Birch, Trembling Aspen.	Columbia	Western Red Cedar, Western Hemlock, Douglas-fir.
Forest and Barren	White Spruce, Black Spruce, Tamarack.	Deciduous	Beech, maple, Black Walnut, hickory, oak.
Forest and Grass	Trembling Aspen, willow.	Great Lakes-St. Lawrence	Red Pine, Eastern White Pine, Yellow Birch, maple, oak.
Subalpine	Engelmann Spruce, Alpine Fir, Lodgepole Pine.	Acadian	Red Spruce, Balsam Fir, maple, Yellow Birch.
Montane	Douglas-fir, Lodgepole and Ponderosa Pine, Trembling Aspen.	The Grasslands	Trembling Aspen, willow, Bur Oak.

HUDSON

BAY

NEWFOUNDLAND

QUEBEC

ONTARIO

NEW
BRUNSWICK

P.E.I.

NOVA
SCOTIA

ATLANTIC

OCEAN

14

15
The Acadian Forest Region, Cape Breton, Nova Scotia

19
The Boreal Forest Region, Riding Mountain National Park, Manitoba

14
The Coast Forest Region, Cathedral Grove, Port Alberni, British Columbia

Canada's Forests are Rich and Varied

Great Lakes-St. Lawrence Forest
on, Gatineau Park, Quebec

17
The Deciduous Forest Region, Hamilton,
Ontario

18
The Subalpine Forest Region, Kootenay
National Park, British Columbia

Grasslands, Upper Qu'Appelle Valley,
atchewan

21
The Columbia Forest Region, Upper Arrow
Lake, British Columbia

22
The Montane Forest Region, Prince George,
British Columbia

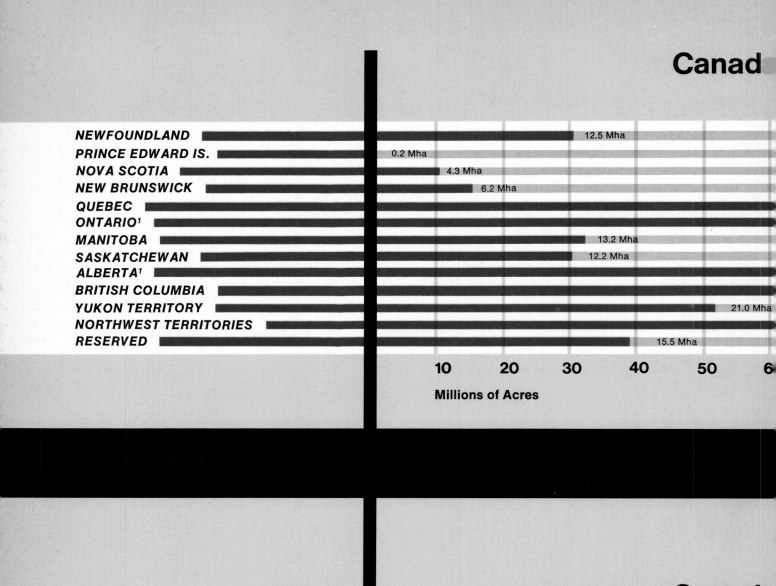

NEWFOUNDLAND	12.5 Mha
PRINCE EDWARD IS.	0.2 Mha
NOVA SCOTIA	4.3 Mha
NEW BRUNSWICK	6.2 Mha
QUEBEC	
ONTARIO[1]	
MANITOBA	13.2 Mha
SASKATCHEWAN	12.2 Mha
ALBERTA[1]	
BRITISH COLUMBIA	
YUKON TERRITORY	21.0 Mha
NORTHWEST TERRITORIES	
RESERVED	15.5 Mha

10 20 30 40 50 6

Millions of Acres

Canada

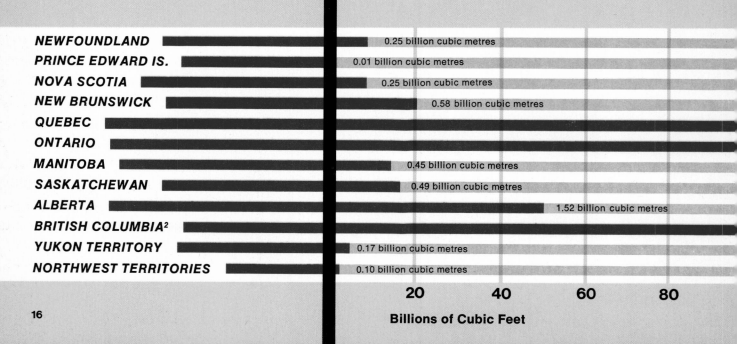

NEWFOUNDLAND	0.25 billion cubic metres
PRINCE EDWARD IS.	0.01 billion cubic metres
NOVA SCOTIA	0.25 billion cubic metres
NEW BRUNSWICK	0.58 billion cubic metres
QUEBEC	
ONTARIO	
MANITOBA	0.45 billion cubic metres
SASKATCHEWAN	0.49 billion cubic metres
ALBERTA	1.52 billion cubic metres
BRITISH COLUMBIA[2]	
YUKON TERRITORY	0.17 billion cubic metres
NORTHWEST TERRITORIES	0.10 billion cubic metres

20 40 60 80

Billions of Cubic Feet

orest Land

.9 Million Acres — 326.1 Million Hectares

Forest land is defined as land capable of producing stands of trees with a minimum diameter breast high (D.B.H.) of 4 inches (or 10 cm) growing on 10 per cent or more of the area. It does not include shelter belts, forest units 5 acres or less in area, or land capable of producing stands as above but currently in agricultural use.

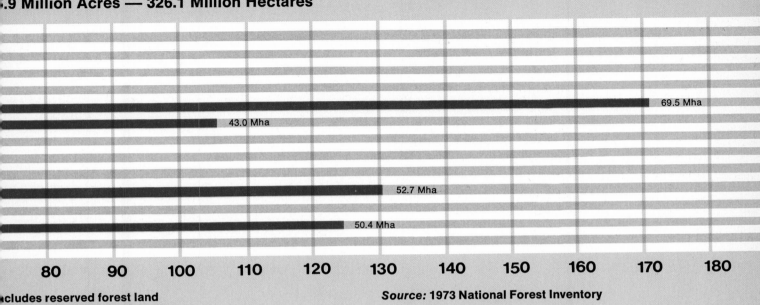

69.5 Mha

43.0 Mha

52.7 Mha

50.4 Mha

80 90 100 110 120 130 140 150 160 170 180

cludes reserved forest land
reakdown not available

Source: 1973 National Forest Inventory

lerchantable Timber[1]

2.6 Billion Cubic Feet — 19.3 Billion Cubic Metres

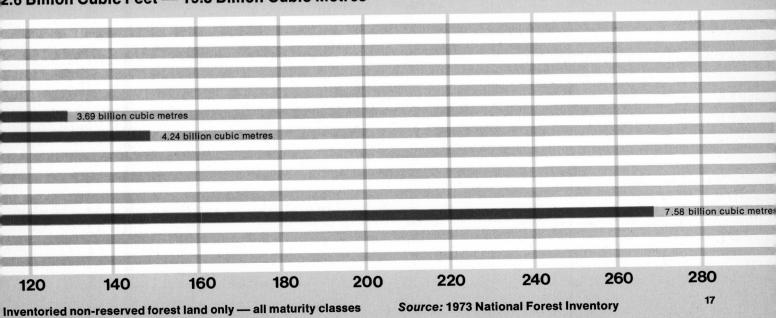

3.69 billion cubic metres

4.24 billion cubic metres

7.58 billion cubic metres

120 140 160 180 200 220 240 260 280

Inventoried non-reserved forest land only — all maturity classes
Mature timber only

Source: 1973 National Forest Inventory

17

The Canadian People Own Most of Canada's Forest Lands

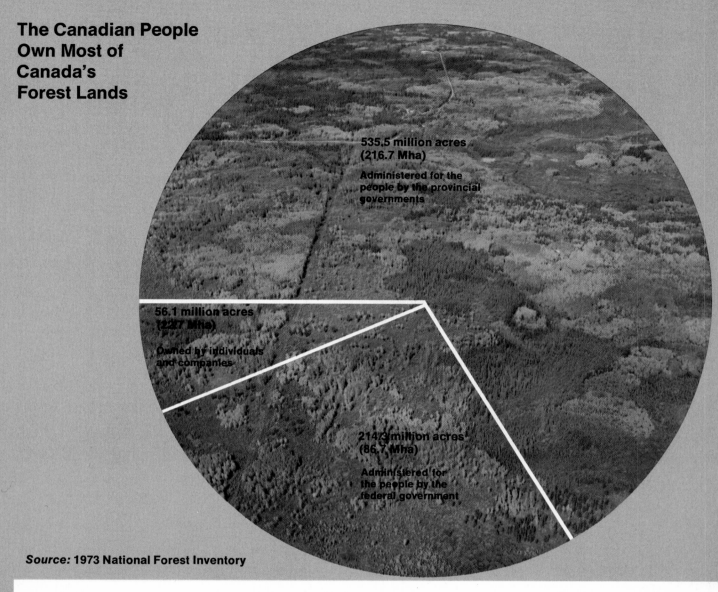

535.5 million acres (216.7 Mha)

Administered for the people by the provincial governments

56.1 million acres (22.7 Mha)

Owned by individuals and companies

214.3 million acres (86.7 Mha)

Administered for the people by the federal government

Source: 1973 National Forest Inventory

Private Forest Land Holdings Vary Considerably Between Provinces*

	Millions of acres	(Millions of hectares)	Private forest land as percentage of total forest land
NEWFOUNDLAND (including Labrador)	1.2	0.5	3.9
PRINCE EDWARD ISLAND	0.6	0.2	94.3
NOVA SCOTIA	7.9	3.2	72.2
NEW BRUNSWICK	8.3	3.4	53.3
QUEBEC	17.9	7.2	10.4
ONTARIO	10.4	4.2	9.7
MANITOBA	0.7	0.3	2.0
SASKATCHEWAN	1.0	0.4	3.1
ALBERTA	1.9	0.8	2.4
BRITISH COLUMBIA	6.3	2.6	4.7

*There are no significant areas of private forest land in the Yukon and Northwest Territories.

Source: 1973 National Forest Inventory

Forest Administration and Policy

By far the greater part of Canada's 805.9 million acres (326.1 Mha) of forest land is owned by her people as a whole and administered by provincial and federal governments. Included in government-administered forest lands are areas set aside as parks, game refuges, water conservation areas, and nature preserves where, by legislation, wood production is not a primary use. Such lands, of course, are for the benefit of all Canadians and are shared as well by increasing numbers of visitors. Only 56.1 million acres (22.7 Mha) of forest land are privately owned.

Each of the provinces has its own forestry agency responsible for managing all forest lands within its boundaries except those which are federally or privately held. This agency is usually a branch or service within a ministry concerned with natural resources. In general, the responsibilities assumed by the provinces are broad and include such aspects as timber disposal; forest inventory; protection against fire, insects, and disease; forest management; extension and infor-

mation services; and in some cases forest research.

The federal government has responsibility for the forest resources of the Yukon and Northwest Territories as well as those on other federal lands such as national parks, Indian reserves, forest experiment stations, and military bases.

The Canadian Forestry Service of the federal Department of the Environment has statutory authority to conduct research and development activities for the benefit of forest management throughout the country. It also provides forestry advice and services to other federal departments. The forest resources of the Yukon and Northwest Territories are the concern of the Department of Indian and Northern Affairs. Parks Canada, a directorate within that department, is responsible for the extensive forest areas within Canada's national parks while the Department of Industry, Trade and Commerce promotes the well-being of forest industries and the marketing of forest products. As part of its policy in handling regional problems, the Department of Regional Economic Expansion provides funds to provincial governments for improvement of Crown forests and also to woodlot owners for upgrading

Provincial governments use every means to apprise the public of the need to protect the country's forests.

24,25
Using a variety of instruments, provincial forestry technicians determine such features as tree height and basal area for forest inventory and management purposes.

26
Economic harvest, good regeneration, and sustained wildlife cover are the concepts guiding the policy of strip clear-cutting on Nova Scotia's Chignecto Management Unit.

24

25

26

27
New Brunswick forestry personnel
check the forest harvest.

28
The Horsefly Ranger Station of the
British Columbia Forest Service in the
Williams Lake area

their properties and developing group management units.

Of Canada's 56.1 million acres (22.7 Mha) of privately owned forest land, 46.3 million acres (18.7 Mha) are located east of Manitoba. Provincial governments seldom exercise direct authority over private forest lands although they may subsidize forest management thereon and also exercise some control through taxation policy, protection regulations, and the work of their forest extension services.

A number of forest industry companies in Canada own large areas of forest land which they seek to manage on a sustained-yield basis. However, there is a growing awareness on the part of these organizations of a need to develop management plans with due regard for environmental factors and other uses of forest land separate from fibre production. Public access, recreation, fishing, hunting, and watershed protection are increasingly being viewed as a legitimate concern of private industry.

During the early settlement of Canada, there were few restrictions on cutting timber other than those that sought to reserve trees suitable for naval requirements. In many situations the forest was simply an impediment to agriculture and, as such, was summarily removed by cutting and burning. With the passage of time wider controls over timber cutting evolved. These ranged from the simple levying of fees for timber cut to the more sophisticated systems of leasing land and disposing of timber which prevail in the provinces today. Most of these methods combine annual charges on an area basis, fees for the quantity of wood cut, and certain requirements with respect to forest protection and forest management. For the most part, leases are of medium length ranging from 10 to 50 years.

British Columbia, developing later than the eastern provinces, has quite an elaborate system of licences through which cutting rights to provincial forests are sold. One of these is the tree-farm licence. In this contract the government leases a specified area of Crown forest land to an individual or company. This land, together with the private holdings, if any, of the individual or company are calculated to sustain a supply of timber sufficient to justify capital outlay for a mill and equipment. Such leases run for 21 years with conditional renewal, and in return for assured supplies of raw

To help in its forest protection operations the Province of Ontario has converted these Grumman Tracker aircraft into fire-fighting airtankers.

material the licensee agrees to participate in such activities as seed collection, planting, inventory, rehabilitation of logged areas, and fire-fighting. He also pays stumpage on the timber cut on public lands.

Many forest policies in Canada are in a state of change. This situation is born of a recent and growing realization of some rather basic facts with respect to the forest resource. Important among these is the need to cope with a growing demand for wood from a finite area of forest land. There is also the matter of increasing public insistence for forests to yield a greater measure of recreation, wildlife, and water values. Then too, the price of forest products has been increasing at a much greater rate than that of the raw material. Some examples of changes or impending changes in forest policy will serve to illustrate the impact of this new set of circumstances.

In Canada's national parks, the right to cut timber for commercial purposes was discontinued under the terms of the 1969 national parks policy, and in 1970-71, all grazing of domestic stock within the parks was also terminated. These actions were taken to help protect and preserve the natural recreational, scenic, and other aesthetic values of the parks.

Steps were taken in 1972 to revise existing federal statutes and regulations relating to the forests of the Yukon and Northwest Territories. This was done in anticipation of an eventual need on the part of forest industry to secure a supply of raw material from hitherto uncommitted areas of productive forest land.

In the provinces, Ontario has adopted a new forest policy aimed at producing 25.8 million cubic metres (911 million cubic feet) of industrial roundwood by the year 2020. To achieve this, plans have been made to double the present level of silvicultural activity with the government accepting full responsibility for the regeneration of cut-over and burned Crown lands.

New Brunswick's forest development plans include a change in Crown land tenure from the existing timber licence system to full control by the province. This guarantees wood supplies to forest-based industries and places higher emphasis on the best use of timber, environmental protection, multiple use, artificial reforestation, and stand improvement.

Saskatchewan's policies are also directed towards greater concern with reforestation as well as stricter utilization standards and certain restrictions on clear cutting.

New forestry legislation and a new forest taxation system are being developed by the Government of Newfoundland. Here too, this will mean greater government involvement in forest management, increased forest utilization, reduction of environmental damage caused by logging, and a greater emphasis on multiple use.

Changes in forest policies in British Columbia are concerned with selling Crown timber for what it is worth — no more and no less. It has been estimated that implementation of all recommended changes will result in an increase of $31 million in provincial revenues. Current policies also pay particular heed to multiple use and the more complete utilization of residues from logging and milling for pulp and paper manufacture.

Sweeping changes being considered by Quebec include repossessing forest concessions, incorporating them into a domainal system, and re-allocating

30
A deputy ranger of the British Columbia Forest Service checks details with a log salvage operator in the Chilliwack area.

resources on a mill-by-mill basis. Stumpage dues may also be abolished to be replaced by a variable fee system which would take account of such factors as the quality of species cut, distance from the mill, operating difficulties, and the prevailing state of the forest industry.

While some common trends in forest policy are developing across Canada, there is, however, no national forest policy. There would appear to be distinct advantages for forest industry, federal and provincial governments, the forestry profession, and the public at large if

such a policy were to emerge. It is noteworthy that the Canadian Council of Resource and Environment Ministers, the Canadian Pulp and Paper Association, the Canadian Institute of Forestry, and the Canadian Forestry Service have all recently evinced interest in this matter.

Forest Protection, Management, and Harvesting

Man Causes Three Out of Four Forest Fires . . .

Annually, some 7 600 fires sweep across an average of almost 2 million acres (0.8 Mha) of forest land in Canada. They claim around 0.3 billion cubic feet (8.5 million cubic metres) of merchantable timber valued in excess of $13 million. This amount of timber would make three Great Pyramids of Khufu with material to spare. No figures are available to tell the story of damage to soils and wildlife or to recreation values and water resources. In recent years, the annual cost of providing fire protection for Canada's forests has averaged in excess of $50 million. Two other interesting facets arise from the statistics. While about 75 per cent of fires are man-caused, the remainder, started by lightning, account for more than half of the total area burned.

Because of the tenure of forest land, the provincial governments are responsible for forest-fire control over most of Canada's productive forests. The federal government is directly concerned with protecting the forests of the Yukon and Northwest Territories as well as those growing on national parks, forest research stations, and other federally owned land. Forest industries play an important role in forest-fire control by training and equipping their employees to fight fires. Irrespective of the agency involved, however, the basic objective is the same: the protection of life, property, and high-value resources. Essentially, the approach is threefold covering prevention, detection, and suppression.

The chances of forest fire occurring are undoubtedly lessened by such current practices as scattering or burning logging slash, restricting public use of wooded areas in times of high or extreme fire hazard, and insisting on spark arrestors for engine-driven machinery. However, probably the single most important fire prevention tool used in Canada is public education.

Man-caused fires originate with recreational users of the forest, land operators, wood operators, railroads, industries, incendiaries, and others. By far

31

33, 34
Both single- and multi-engined air-tankers are used in Canada. Some carry water in the floats, others within the fuselage. Float planes and amphibians are able to fill their tanks automatically during taxi runs on lakes or rivers. Upper — The amphibious Canadair CL 215, designed and built in Canada specifically as an airtanker. Lower — A De Havilland Turbo-Beaver with floats adapted for fire-fighting.

32

32
Helicopters with special buckets can load water quickly from local lakes or rivers and spot-bomb fires in early stages. They are also used to ferry fire-fighters and equipment directly to an outbreak.

31
Decades of growth succumb in mere seconds to the onslaught of fire.

33

34

35
The Avenger, a World War II torpedo bomber, is a popular land-based air-tanker. Chemical fire retardants added to the water are also fertilizers and may have a beneficial effect on burn sites. Red colouring mixed with the load helps the pilot check on drop accuracy.

36
Many fire lookout towers are still manned, but aircraft are proving cheaper and just as efficient for fire detection.

36

the most significant of these groups is the first one. Campers, hunters, anglers, hikers, and forest vacationers were responsible for over 23 per cent of man-made forest fires over a recent 10-year period.

Every forest-fire protection organization in Canada engages in some aspect of public education to make all these people aware of the rules of fire safety in the forest. Television, radio, films, and roadside fire-danger warnings are all used. The Canadian Forestry Association, a nation-wide, non-profit, forest conservation group, emphasizes fire prevention in its annual National Forest Week and keeps Smokey Bear, the cartoon character fire-prevention symbol, prominent in the public eye.

Effective fire-control planning and operations in all parts of Canada are greatly assisted by a fire-danger rating system developed over the years by the Canadian Forestry Service. This system, published as the Canadian Forest Fire Weather Index, contains a number of indices designed to facilitate the prediction of fire occurrence and behaviour. It is based on daily noontime observations of temperature, relative humidity, windspeed, and 24-hour rainfall. The publication guides such provincial actions as

concentrating aircraft patrols, airtankers, and fire-fighters in high hazard areas; increasing standby fire-fighting personnel; withdrawing burning permits; issuing forest travel permits; or enforcing forest closure.

Aircraft have played an increasingly prominent role in detecting forest fires in Canada since they were first tried for this purpose in 1920. In comparison with tower lookout networks they have proved more economical and equally effective. Besides visual spotting by pilots and observers, some aircraft are now equipped with an infrared scanner which assists fire-fighters by plotting fire boundaries even through dense smoke. Computers, too, have recently been used to aid aerial detection. Drawing on information related to such matters as forest fuels, thunderstorm paths, historical fire data, and the availability of aircraft and finances, the computer is quickly able to establish the aerial patrol routes which will yield the best detection results. Despite the effective use of aircraft and fire towers, however, many forest fires are still spotted and reported first by observant, quick-thinking members of the general public.

Probably the most spectacular advance in forest-fire suppression in

Canada has resulted from the use of airtankers for dropping water and chemical fire retardants. First tried here in 1945, this technique is now widely used across the country. Many different types of aircraft and many different methods of discharging water or retardant solutions on fire sites have been tried. Early spotting, followed by prompt aerial attack frequently results in successful containment until ground crews with conventional equipment can reach the site.

The basic approach to fire-fighting on the ground has not changed greatly with the years. Encirclement, construction of fire lines, and use of the backfire are still standard procedures. But considerable progress has been made in providing better tools for the job, in transporting men to and from the fire line, and in providing on-the-spot radio communication.

Hand tools are used in nearly all fires. Among these is the backpack fire pump, a Canadian invention of the early 1920's. In 1915, the first portable gasoline-powered fire pumps were also pioneered in Canada. Today's fire-fighters move into action with modern versions of these units on their backs. The small, rugged pumps develop pressures in excess of 200 pounds per square inch (1380 kPa) and with their special hoses they are particularly effective when water sources are located within reasonable range of a fire. Such pumps may also be operated in relay to deliver water over distances of a mile (1.6 km) or more. Where access permits, men, equipment, water, and chemicals are trucked to the fire and heavy equipment is used to clear and plough fire breaks.

Not so many years ago, fires in remote, inaccessible areas could only be left to burn; but aircraft have changed this situation. Float planes are often able to use the lakes of the northern forests to deliver suppression crews to within striking distance of an outbreak and helicopters may also transport fire-fighters directly to a fire site.

Light-weight, efficient, two-way radios now permit a fire boss to keep in constant contact with all units of his fire-control force as well as his headquarters. This is of inestimable value in marshalling his resources against an enemy as dangerous and unpredictable as the forest fire. The day is also not far distant when co-ordinated forest-fire management systems will emerge. Such systems will effectively combine computers and human fire-fighting expertise to give quick, added strength to many aspects of the battle against forest fire.

Fire has influenced forest patterns from earliest times and observation has led to a fund of knowledge concerning both long- and short-term changes that can be expected in the wake of a conflagration. In one instance fire may prove to be a step in converting a decadent, low-value forest into a vigorous new stand, while in another case it may represent a devastating economic loss of prime timber or a catastrophic blow to a valuable water-supply catchment. Appreciation of the role of fire with respect to specific forests will thus influence fire-control planning and priorities.

It has also been logical to move from the observed effects of wildfire to the use of prescribed (controlled) fire to achieve certain management goals. So far, most prescribed fires have been used for the removal of hazardous slash in British Columbia. Such fires, however, often meet a secondary objective by preparing the way for both natural and artificial regeneration. This is accomplished not only by slash removal but also through the release of nutrients and the optimum exposure of mineral soil.

37
Prescribed fire, such as this one in Ontario, helps an experienced forest manager to prepare a site for planting or seeding, to remove hazardous slash, or perhaps control an insect or disease outbreak. Its size, intensity, and rate of spread are fully controlled.

38
Although natural fire may seldom coincide with man's plans, it sometimes shortens the gap between a decadent forest and a vigorous new stand.

39
In spite of assistance from aircraft and heavy ground equipment, fire-fighting is still a matter of back-breaking toil, sweat, and personal danger.

Some Common Forest Enemies

40
Spruce budworm moth and pupa

40

42
Forest tent caterpillar

41
Larch sawfly larva

41

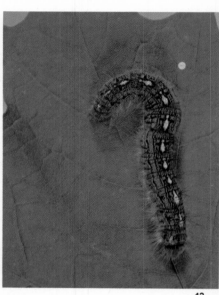

42

43 **43**
White pine weevil

44 **44**
Hemlock looper

Controlling Forest Pests-
The Delicate War
with Selective Weapons . . .

Historically, insects and diseases, along with fire and windstorms, have always taken their toll of the forest, but this has been simply an integral part of the slow, natural pattern of forest succession. In the early days of settlement, when human demands on the forest were slight, such inroads were of little consequence. In this century, however, man has necessarily entered into serious competition with Nature's forest harvesting methods both to ensure a supply of industrial products and to maintain desirable recreational areas. Modern methods of detection and control are now accomplishing much towards keeping insect and disease damage within acceptable limits.

All of Canada's forest lands are subject to a continuing surveillance with respect to forest insect and disease conditions. This work, which is the responsibility of the Forest Insect and Disease Survey of the Canadian Forestry Service, is conducted in close collaboration with provincial government forest agencies, forest industries, and a number of private organizations. Early detection and prompt reporting of insect and disease outbreaks, the prime function of the Survey, greatly enhance prospects for control.

Because of the many and complex problems that may arise in combatting forest pests, Canada also operates the Annual Forest Pest Control Forum under the aegis of the Canadian Forestry Service. This Forum provides an opportunity for representatives of provincial and federal governments and private agencies to foregather and review research and operations related to forest pest control.

Aerial spraying of chemical insecticides has proved so far to be the most effective means of gaining control over injurious forest insects. The knowledge gained of the toxic effects of DDT on birds, sports fish, and invertebrates, coupled with an appreciation of its role in the global environment led to the end of the use of this chemical in the fight against Canadian forest insect pests. Since 1965, however, many compounds have been evaluated as replacements for DDT. Prominent among those adopted for regular spraying have been fenitrothion, phosphamidon, Matacil, and Zectran. Any material designated for use in insect control must first satisfy certain federal and provincial regulations before

45

45

The Canadair CL 215 is used in Canada
both for forest insecticide spraying
and fire-fighting.

it passes from the experimental to the operational phase.

The spruce budworm is recognized as the most widely distributed destructive forest insect pest of North America. In Canada, in 1974, this insect, which favours spruces, firs, and Douglas-fir, caused moderate to severe defoliation over some 115 million acres (46.5 Mha). Damage was concentrated in eastern Canada particularly in Quebec, Ontario, New Brunswick, and Newfoundland with

smaller areas affected in Nova Scotia and Prince Edward Island. Defoliation was also reported in southern British Columbia, northern Alberta, and parts of southern Manitoba.

In the past several years, the greater part of funds and effort for forest insect spray operations has been spent in eastern Canada on the spruce budworm. The work has been concentrated on large forest tracts in Quebec and New Brunswick and on certain relatively

 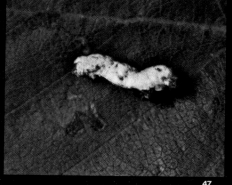 

46, 47
A birch sawfly larva succumbs to fungous attack.

46

47

48
Jack pine sawfly larvae killed by a virus

48

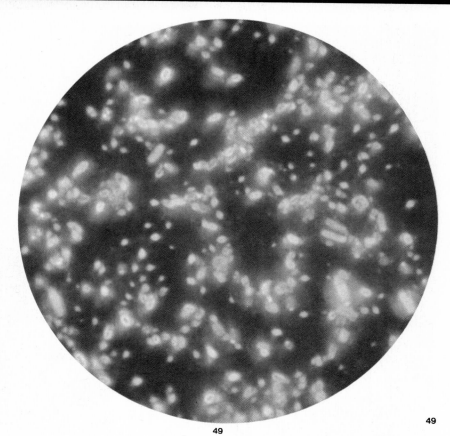

49

In this *Bacillus thuringiensis* culture the bacteria appear light green, spores are bright red, and protein crystals are bright yellow. These crystals, produced when the bacteria form spores, are toxic to most moth and butterfly larvae including the spruce budworm.

49

small but important recreational areas in Ontario.

Although biological control of insect pests has received a great deal of study in Canada, it has not provided answers on the same scale as in the case of the chemical pesticides. However, biological approaches, with their greater specificity as to target insects, have considerable potential in terms of achieving control with a minimum disruption of the environment. Insect parasites, predators, and pathogens have all been used against forest insects.

One of the most successful early cases of biological control was achieved through the combined action of two released parasites and an accidentally introduced virus disease against the European spruce sawfly. It has been estimated that this pest, regarded as a major threat to eastern Canadian spruce forests during the 1930's, was responsible for killing some 8.5 million cords (30.8 million cubic metres [stacked]) on the Gaspé Peninsula. The outbreak collapsed by 1945 and thereafter the virus and the parasites have combined to keep the sawfly numbers at a level where they no longer have economic significance. More recently introduced parasites have proved effective in the control of winter moth which is found mainly in Nova Scotia.

Predators have been less effective than parasites as control agents. Many species of predators have been introduced against the balsam woolly aphid but results have been consistently disappointing.

In the field of pathogens, viruses and bacteria have shown the greatest promise although there is also potential for the use of fungi and protozoa. The introduced virus of the European spruce sawfly has already been mentioned, but it is known that viruses also attack other sawflies as well as the Lepidoptera (moths and butterflies). Work on a virus affecting the Swaine jack pine sawfly has resulted in the isolation of a more virulent strain which causes 90 per cent mortality in larvae and operational aerial applications have yielded promising results.

By far the best-known insect pathogen among the bacteria is *Bacillus thuringiensis*. This species produces a substance toxic to a wide range of Lepidoptera larvae. Special *B. thuringiensis* formulations are commercially available and recently improved products have been extensively tested in aerial applications against spruce budworm in Quebec, Ontario, and Manitoba and against the false western hemlock looper in British Columbia. Significant reduction of these pests was achieved in the tests and operational spray programmes against spruce budworm are now proceeding.

Other biological control agents receiving attention in Canada are sex attractants or pheromones, and growth regulators or hormones. Although much research is still needed, present evidence suggests that pheromones may eventually be used to trap or confuse the males of insect pest species and thus restrict mating and achieve significant population reductions. Along similar lines, hormones have now been syn-

50
Hypoxylon canker on trembling aspen

50

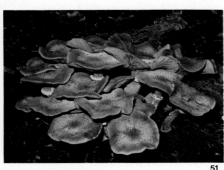

51
Mushroom of the armillaria root rot fungus

51

52
White pine blister rust

52

53
White elm killed by Dutch elm disease

53

54
Dwarf mistletoe, a parasitic plant

54

55

55

In western Canada, conifers, particularly lodgepole pine, are often damaged and sometimes destroyed by a weather-related phenomenon known as "Red Belt" which turns the foliage reddish-brown. The precise cause is not known but it appears to be related to rapid temperature changes during winter months.

56
A "shark-finned" barrel scarifier used in site preparation

thesized that prevent an insect from reaching its adult reproductive stage. Tests of aerial applications of certain of these hormones are being made against the eastern hemlock looper and the spruce budworm.

Control of forest diseases has not proved to be a simple matter. Only in isolated instances does there appear to be a place for chemical sprays which have proved so effective against insects. The approach to disease control is generally limited to various forest management practices. These may include such actions as minimizing tree damage to reduce disease entry, removing infected trees or tree parts to prevent spread, or, perhaps, eradicating intermediate hosts to disrupt the life cycle of a disease organism. Breeding of disease-resistant trees may also be a solution.

Heart rot, which is caused by a number of different fungi, is the pre-eminent tree disease in Canada. It is estimated that almost 1 billion cubic feet (28.3 million cubic metres) of merchantable timber are lost to heart rot annually. Careful logging practices, aimed at leaving standing trees undamaged, together with early harvesting of damaged trees are useful controls. The disease is more serious in older trees and can be expected to decrease considerably as mature and overmature stands are logged and second growth is cut on shorter rotation.

Probably the best-known tree disease in Canada is the Dutch elm disease. First observed in Canada in 1944, it has become a serious pest of native elm trees in Quebec, Ontario, and New Brunswick. A fungus carried by bark beetles invades the vascular system of the trees, impedes water movement, and causes death. The slow but steady advance of the disease threatens the continued existence of elm trees which are favoured ornamentals as well as being a valuable timber-producing species in some areas. The removal of infected trees, spraying to prevent bark beetle feeding, and the introduction of chemicals into the trees to prevent or arrest disease development or to kill the beetles, have all been tried. So far, no truly effective, economical method has been discovered to either prevent or control the disease over the wide areas affected.

Forest Management Reaches for New Concepts, New Techniques . . .

In the early days of Canada's history, the emphasis was on the utilization of the forests and the removal of the best trees. There was little understanding of, or concern for, the long-term productivity of the forest. During the second half of the 19th century attitudes began to change. The diminishing supply of high-quality white pine in eastern Canada proved that even in those seemingly limitless forests serious shortages could occur. This concern was eventually expressed in the concept of sustained yield — the idea, in its narrowest sense, of managing the forest to ensure that the amount of wood cut from a given area over a given time does not exceed the quantity produced in the same period. Wood removed according to this plan is called the allowable cut. In essence, sustained yield was accepted as a guiding principle in forest management across the country. However, over the years, the concept has assumed a certain vagueness and some economists and foresters now challenge it as being outdated in terms of current economics and integrated resource management.

Canada is now cutting approximately 4.5 billion cubic feet (127 million cubic metres) of wood annually. It has been estimated that by the year 2000 there will be an annual demand for 7.6 billion cubic feet (215 million cubic metres) which is approaching the estimated annual allowable cut of about 8.5 billion

56

57
Bare-root tree planting operations

58
Walters' bullets, now made from biodegradable plastic, were an early container-planting development in Canada.

58

57

cubic feet (241 million cubic metres) on inventoried productive timber lands. To provide the necessary wood for the future and take full advantage of the economic benefits that appear to be in store, there is a need for all cut-over and burned-over areas to be returned expeditiously to maximum production. There is also a need for improvement of existing forest stands. These matters are receiving increasing attention across the country.

The challenge of forest regeneration is formidable. About 2.25 million acres (0.91 Mha) of forest land are harvested annually. On the average, almost as much again is lost to fire and there is also a backlog of 42 million acres (17 Mha) inadequately regenerated following fire and unsuccessful farming attempts.

Scarification, herbicides, and prescribed fire (mentioned earlier) are all used in Canada as methods of preparing cut-over and other sites for regeneration. In some cases these measures simply aid regeneration arising from natural seed-fall; in others they prepare the way for planting or seeding operations.

Considerable effort has gone into the

production of equipment for scarifying and Ontario has been prominent in this field. Various tractor-drawn ploughs, rakes, finned barrels, rolling choppers, and spiked anchor chains are some of the items used on slash, brush, and duff to expose areas of mineral soil which are receptive to seeding and planting.

Herbicides have proved useful in suppressing grass and woody plants that otherwise would have been heavy competition for establishing trees. Aerial application of herbicides has also been used to release coniferous regeneration from beneath shrub cover and hardwood canopies.

About 290 000 acres (117 000 ha) are planted to trees annually in Canada using bare-root nursery stock for over 90 per cent of the operation. Although some mud-packed seedlings are used in British Columbia, most of the balance of planting stock is produced in a variety of individual containers. In some cases, both seedling and container are planted while in other techniques the seedling encased in its moulded rooting medium is removed from the container and planted separately.

While planting machines are used to some extent in most provinces, by far the larger part of the bare-root stock is hand planted because of the wide-

59

spread rugged terrain and rocky soils encountered on Canadian forest sites. A number of hand tools have already been devised for planting container stock, but recent developments suggest that both container seedling production and planting operations will eventually be mechanized with consequent added savings over bare-root planting methods. Adverse site conditions will, of course, also impose limits on mechanized container planting.

Direct seeding for forest regeneration in Canada has increased considerably in recent years to the point where more than 60 000 acres (24 000 ha) are seeded annually. Spiralling costs of bare-root stock coupled with labour shortages have contributed to this increase. Despite this present trend, hoped-for levels of stocking have only been achieved with jack pine.

An important aspect of artificial regeneration work is highly developed nursery and greenhouse programmes capable of producing good-quality material as bare-root or containerized planting stock. While Canada already possesses many such facilities, they can be expected to grow in numbers in response to expanding regeneration demands.

Closely related to the ultimate success of nursery and greenhouse work is the

60

59
Using a specially designed "gun", over 2300 bullet seedlings can be planted per man-day.

60
A close-up view of a container seedling produced by the increasingly popular, Canadian-developed styroblock method

62
The special attachment at the rear of
this oversnow vehicle is used to
broadcast tree seed.

62

61
Tree planting machine in operation
in Quebec

61

matter of tree improvement. Most reforestation authorities in Canada have now
adopted the seed-zone principle where-
by forest areas with uniform environment
are delimited. When seedlings are grown
in the zone from which the parent seed
was harvested, advantage is taken of natural selection processes, which, over
long periods, have adapted the trees to
local conditions. Within seed zones, further genetic improvement is achieved by
establishing seed-production areas consisting of stands chosen for their above-
average qualities and managing these
exclusively for seed production. Special
seed orchards, offering even greater genetic advances, are on the increase in
Canada. Such plantations draw on the
best parent material in a seed zone and
may be propagated from cuttings, grafts,
or seed. They are isolated to reduce pol-
lination from inferior outside sources and
are intensively managed to produce the
best seed crops.

Forest improvement work involving
fertilizers and thinning is receiving considerable attention in Canada although
operational management programmes
are as yet by no means widespread.

Field trials with nitrogen and nitrogen/
phosphorus fertilizers have resulted in

63

63
On Nova Scotia's Stanley Forest Management Unit, superior stands of red
pine have been thinned and fertilized
to establish a natural seed-production
area for an expanding reforestation
effort.

65
Loading urea fertilizer aboard a helicopter for application on Laval University's Montmorency Research Forest

64
Grafting operations in the production of blister-rust-resistant white pine

66
Pre-commercial thinning by machine in a high-density, 10-year-old jack pine stand

substantial growth increases for a number of tree species, and the potential value of forest fertilizing does not appear to be in question. However, the use of fertilizer as a means of increasing production in the adult forest has been delayed by the relative ease of acquiring added volumes of wood by the simple expedient of cutting more trees. In addition, difficulties have been encountered in achieving quick development of economic and environmentally safe fertilizing procedures. Operational programmes of forest fertilizing commenced around 1962 and to date a total of between 20 000 and 30 000 acres (8 000 and 12 000 ha) have been treated. Largest operations have been in British Columbia where Douglas-fir has been the main species fertilized.

Little commercial thinning is practised in Canada but there have been developments in pre-commercial thinning, sometimes referred to as spacing or cleaning. Unlike commercial thinning, this treatment does not yield an immediate harvest of merchantable material, but simply reduces competition in dense young stands. This, in turn, results in shorter rotation periods and lower harvesting costs.

Pre-commercial thinning is carried out regularly in several provinces but Quebec is most heavily involved with an annual

programme encompassing about 40 000
acres (16 000 ha). Most thinning operations are done manually by chemical injection or by cutting with a variety of tools
ranging from axes and brush hooks to
power circular brush saws and chain
saws. However, these labour-intensive
methods are slow and costly, and mechanized strip thinning, using specially
designed mowers and drum choppers,
is receiving increasing attention in areas
where surface conditions permit its use.

An inventory of the forest resource is
a basic tool for effective planning and
management. Virtually all of Canada's
forests have now been covered by some
type of inventory and for many inventoried areas work is progressing on more
intensive and up-to-date surveys.

Primary responsibility for compiling
forest inventories rests with the provinces. The federal role relates to research, development, advisory services,
forest surveys on federal lands, and col-
lation of data for the national forest inventory. The national inventory covers
the area and tenure of forest land, the
merchantable timber by province and
maturity class, and forest depletion by
harvesting and fire.

While a variety of inventory techniques
are employed by the provinces, all make
extensive use of aerial photographs,
most taken specifically for forest inventory purposes. Panchromatic or modi-
fied infrared photographs at a scale of
1:15,840 are widely used but smaller
scales of 1:50,000 are sometimes preferred for broad forest typing or the in-
terpretation of site productivity. Colour
photography is sometimes used on special projects.

Impressive new tools with potential
for forest inventory work and general
resource appraisal are also appearing.
Large-scale (1:500 to 1:3,000) aerial
photography, used in conjunction with
tilt measurement devices and a radar
altimeter recently developed to meet
Canadian Forestry Service specifications
by Canada's National Research Council,
is proving to be excellent for detailed
forest inventory sampling. There are also
strong indications that satellites will be
used in the future. Promising material
produced by the Landsat Programme is
already being evaluated for use in forest
appraisal work as well as in the assessment of wildlife habitat and water
resources.

Other useful inventory and planning
aids in the shape of improved tables for
predicting timber yield and establishing
timber volumes in plantations and natural
stands have recently been produced in
Canada. Planned metric conversion is
also expected to be accompanied by a
beneficial standardization of the widely
varying methods of measuring primary wood products that have prevailed
across the country.

An important adjunct to forest inventory
is Canada's unique system of surveying
land according to its capability for supporting agriculture, forestry, wildlife, and
recreational activities. This survey, known
as the Canada Land Inventory, commenced in 1963 and embraces approximately 1 million square miles (2.6 million square kilometres), mainly in the
settled areas. It provides maps specifically designed to assist in land use and
resource planning. For forestry, map-
ping is accomplished through interpre-
tation of aerial photographs as well as
field surveys, and the seven capability
classes used indicate the varying capacity of the land to grow commercial timber of identified species.

A New Breed of Logger is at Work in the Woods . . .

One of the most fascinating aspects of the forestry scene in Canada is that of logging, or forest harvesting, to give it its more modern name. Traditionally the domain of the burly lumberjack, famed for his prowess with doubled-bitted axe and saw, Canada's forests now find a new breed of logger abroad in the woods. He is the man behind the pulsing power chain saw; the jockey of a bouncing, articulated rubber-tired skidder, the cab-isolated operator of a multi-armed machine that fells, limbs, bucks, and hauls pulpwood; and he is the man who controls the cable-yarding, radio-controlled, skycrane that lifts logs from the stump area and lofts them up or down slope to the loading area or landing.

Forest harvesting takes in more than simply felling the timber. It covers the whole process of converting trees to sawlogs and pulpwood and delivering the material to the mills. It is dominated by two major concerns. The job must be done as economically as possible and it must be accomplished with an eye to-

wards maintaining wood supplies. Increasingly, too, the methods of forest harvesting are responding to public pressures which are demanding more of the forest than simply wood and fibre.

The most widely adopted pattern of forest harvesting in Canada is that of the clear-cut where all usable timber is removed in one operation. In some areas, more particularly in mixedwood stands or stands of uneven age, selection cutting is practised. Suitable trees are harvested and the resultant thinning effect encourages growth in those that remain.

Systems of forest harvesting vary considerably across Canada in relation to such things as tree size, topography, soil type, and so on. In coastal British Columbia, the area of Canada's forest giants such as the Douglas-fir, western red cedar, and western hemlock, the basic requirement is to harvest sawlogs for the lumber mills. Much of the raw material for the pulp and paper mills of this region comes from sawmill residues, rather than from pulpwood logs.

In the British Columbia coast forest, felling and bucking (that is, the sawing of logs to required length) is done by power chain saw, and in non-mountainous areas skidders, generally specially designed rubber-tired wheel tractors, are used to drag logs from stump to loading area or

68

70

A faller prepares to lay low a Douglas-fir giant in the British Columbia forest.

69

Cable-yarding operations in the British Columbia mountains. Across the valley is the typical pattern left by this system of logging.

70

A radio-controlled skyline crane system at work in the forests of Newfoundland. Transporting logs clear of the ground reduces soil erosion hazards.

69

71
Loading and trucking sawlogs in
British Columbia
72
Loading and trucking pulpwood in
Ontario
73
Flat rafts are a familiar sight in the
sheltered waters of the British
Columbia coast.

landing. However, much of this region is too steep and rugged for the skidders to operate effectively and under these conditions the approach known as cable yarding is employed.

Essentially cable-yarding systems require a tall spar tree or a metal mast which carries cables stretching back to anchor points at the limit of the area to be logged. The commonest form of cable yarding is the highlead where, by means of short choker cables, logs are attached to the mainline cable and winched in along the ground from stump to landing. A variation of cable yarding is the skyline system in which logs are attached to a carriage which moves back and forth on a suspended cable. In some designs it is possible to skid logs for considerable distances along the ground at right angles to the carriage, then hoist them aloft and carry them clear of the ground to the landing.

Less conventional logging methods have also been attempted in British Columbia, more particularly in an effort to overcome difficult terrain and in a measure to respond to environmental concerns. Balloon logging, for example, shows great promise but still requires considerable development work on balloon and yarder design. In tests, helicopter logging has proved to be technically feasible although it is costly and highly energy-consuming. It is believed that this technique will find use only in limited, specialized logging applications.

Trucking of logs is a matter of big business and big machines, particularly in British Columbia. Most logging operations use various types of tractors and cranes with special grapples and booms to pile logs onto the trucks at the landings for forwarding to tidewater and sometimes directly to the mill. Logging trucks are in operation which will haul loads up to 200 tons (181 t).

Logs delivered to tidewater find their way to the mills by rafting and barging. In sheltered waters most logs are moved in flat rafts towed by tugs. These rafts consist of floating logs placed parallel and held together in sections by boom sticks. Over longer distances and under more exposed conditions, self-loading and self-dumping log barges now ply British Columbia's coastal waters. These barges have replaced the piled and lashed ocean-going Davis rafts which presented problems in bad weather and were costly to build and take apart. In addition, barging has reduced log damage by shipworms as well as log loss in transit.

Eastward from coastal British Colum-

73

bia, the forests of Canada produce smaller trees and forest-harvesting methods differ accordingly and are more directly related to the production of pulpwood.

As in the British Columbia coastal area, the logger still operates in the woods with his power chain saw to fell the trees. He may leave them as full trees or delimbed tree lengths to be skidded to the logging road or alternatively he may buck delimbed trees to specified lengths and pile the logs in the stump area. In this case the wood is usually picked up by a wheeled or tracked vehicle called a forwarder and delivered to the landing. Full trees or tree-length logs may be further processed at the roadside into pulpwood or sawlogs by delimbing and slashing machines. In some instances tree-length logs may also be transported to the mill site before further processing occurs.

But while the man with the chain saw still works in the woods, his services are becoming increasingly difficult to obtain. In spite of notable improvements in logging camps and commuting services in some areas, forest operators are struggling to compete with the urban environment for needed labour.

Partly as an outcome of this labour

74
The latest development in ocean transport of logs; the self-loading, self-dumping, and self-propelled "Haida Monarch" operating along the British Columbia coast

75
Pulpwood or sawlogs are cut from tree-lengths and then piled by this mobile slasher.

76

76
Not far removed from science fiction, this three-armed machine operates in eastern Canada to cut and delimb trees. It also reduces them to pulpwood lengths, piles them in the rumble seat, and delivers them to the logging road.

77
A main highway for the white pine square timber trade of the 19th century, the Ottawa River still plays a part for modern forest industry.

77

situation, dramatic advances have been made on mechanizing eastern Canadian forest-harvesting operations. The advent of the hydraulic tree shear, in particular, has brought major changes. In effect a giant pair of scissors capable of snipping off trees close to the ground, the shear has formed the basis of a number of harvesting machines, the most sophisticated of which can carry out all the operations required to reduce a standing tree to pulpwood logs — and deliver them to the roadside. Such machines do the work of many men and also offer challenge and incentive to youth to go to the woods and become highly skilled operators.

Other harvesting developments include the recent introduction of machines for converting whole trees to chips either in the woods or at the mill. Whole-tree chipping, still in its infancy, offers increases of 80 to 100 per cent in wood-fibre production per acre. Although pipelines to transport wood chips are technically feasible, they are not regarded as economically sound at the present time.

East of the Rockies, wood is transported to the mills by river drive, truck, rail, and ship or various combinations of these methods. Approximately 44 per cent of the harvest in eastern Canada still makes at least part of its journey to the mills in the spring of the year via countless streams, rivers, and lakes. The largest river drive in the world is found on Quebec's St. Maurice River where more than 1 million cords (3.6 million cubic metres [stacked]) move downstream each year to feed the mills at La Tuque, Grand'Mère, Shawinigan, and Trois Rivières.

Longer logging seasons, improved logging roads, and better trucks have been responsible for a trend towards increased road transportation. At the same time the proportion of wood moved by river drive and by rail is declining.

78

7

The Productive Forest

78
Logging Industry
79
Wood Industries
80
Paper and Allied Industries
81
Christmas Trees
82
Maple Syrup

80

Wood from Canada's forests is extracted in great abundance and converted into an impressive array of products. Lumber, paper, synthetic fabrics, and many other items have long since become essential to the life styles adopted by a significant portion of the world's population — a population which, we are constantly reminded, is expanding and placing unprecedented strains on both renewable and non-renewable resources.

This situation is at once a blessing and a challenge to Canada, which has within her boundaries approximately 10 per cent of the world's productive forest lands. It is a blessing in that the demand for continued supplies of forest products is expected to expand with a consequent strengthening of trade. It is a challenge because it is already foreseen that by the year 2000 or thereabouts the volume of wood required will approach Canada's currently calculated total allowable cut and eventually the depletion and renewal of the forest must balance on a nationwide scale. The management required to achieve this delicate balance will also have to take account of all other forest uses which are calculated to escalate in importance in response to internal demand. Finally, timing is important. It takes decades for the tree crop to mature and what is done, or not done now, will materially influence the outcome many years hence.

It is against this background that Canada, a forest nation, seeks to provide herself and her trading partners with a continuing wealth of forest products. Viewed nationally, British Columbia, Quebec, and Ontario are the leading provinces with respect to the volume of forest products produced. However, forestry also plays a major role in the economies of the eastern provinces of New Brunswick, Newfoundland, and Nova Scotia.

81

82

Canada's Major Forest Industries . . .

use approximately 4.5 billion cubic feet (127 million cubic metres) of wood annually,
pay $2.792 billion in salaries and wages to 300 000 workers,
export $4.595 billion worth of products representing 18.6 per cent of total domestic exports.*

To provide a clearer impression of the diversity and importance of the major forest industries, they are presented in three main sections: the logging industry, the wood industries, and the paper and allied industries.

The Logging Industry . . .
pays $606 million in salaries and wages to 57 600 workers,
ships $2.494 billion worth of products,
exports $47 million worth of logs, pulpwood, and pulpwood chips.

Logging, or forest harvesting, has been discussed in some detail in the preceding section since it is at once a part of the general forest management pattern as well as being the initial step in almost all forest industry processes.

Canada's three ranking timber-producing provinces are British Columbia, Quebec, and Ontario. These provinces accounted for 49, 20, and 13 per cent, respectively, of the total wood cut in Canada in 1973.

Exports of primary products such as logs, bolts, pulpwood, and pulpwood chips represent a very small portion of the total production of the logging industry. In 1974, Japan and the U.S.A. took almost all of Canada's log exports. In the same year about 85 per cent of pulpwood exports and virtually all pulpwood chip exports went to the U.S.A.

The Wood Industries . . .
pay $938 million in salaries and wages to 119 300 workers,
ship $4.056 billion worth of products,
export $1.873 billion worth of products.

Canada's wood industries are grouped into primary and secondary categories. The primary industries which use roundwood as raw material are the sawmills and planing mills, veneer and plywood plants, shingle mills, and particle board plants. The secondary industries (presented here as one group following the particle board plants) further manufacture part of the output of the primary industries into a wide-ranging assortment of end products such as flooring, doors, sashes, boxes, barrels, and caskets.

*Throughout this chapter, unless otherwise stated, figures refer to 1973.

Sawmills and Planing Mills . . .
pay $554 million in salaries and wages to 62 500 workers,
ship $2.559 billion worth of products,
export $1.598 billion worth of lumber.

The sawmill and planing mill industry is by far the most important component in the primary sector. Recent requirements for greater capital investment in modern, labour-saving mill equipment to cope with rising labour costs has produced a marked movement away from small, seasonally operated mills to larger, highly mechanized establishments running year-round on two and sometimes three shifts. In the 1961-1973 period the number of sawmills and planing mills decreased from 3467 to 1519.

Sixty-eight per cent of lumber, the chief product of this industry, is shipped from British Columbia mills. Spruce is the predominant Canadian softwood lumber species, followed by hemlock and then Douglas-fir. Maple leads among the hardwoods with yellow birch in second place.

The lumber export market is dominated by shipments to the U.S.A. which, in 1974, absorbed 78 per cent of total export volumes. The United Kingdom and Japan are also major lumber customers. The 8.3 billion board feet (37.6 million cubic metres) of lumber exported in 1974 represents sufficient material to build approximately 1.3 million 3-bedroom, single-family dwellings.

Veneer and Plywood Plants . . .
pay $127 million in salaries and wages to 14 500 workers,
ship $487 million worth of products,
export $127 million worth of products.

Softwood veneers and plywoods come almost exclusively from British Columbia and, while hemlock, balsam fir, spruce, and pine are all used by the industry, it is the straight-grained, large-diameter Douglas-fir logs that make up the bulk of the raw material. The production of hardwood veneers and plywoods is confined largely to Canada's eastern provinces and yellow birch is the species most widely used.

A large part of plywood produced is consumed in Canada together with a substantial portion of softwood veneer production. Hardwood veneer, on the other hand, is almost all exported. The United Kingdom took 62 per cent of Canada's plywood exports in 1974. Other major customers were the U.S.A., the Netherlands, and West Germany. In the same year over 90 per cent of veneer exported went to the U.S.A.

Shingle Mills . . .

pay $18 million in salaries and wages to 1900 workers,

ship $68 million worth of products.

This industry covers establishments that produce both shingles and shakes as their major activity. It is concentrated in British Columbia where the straight-growing, easy-splitting western red cedar tree is used as raw material.

The total production of shingles and shakes is not accurately known because considerable quantities are produced as secondary items of manufacture in other industries. Then, too, there is no record of production by small organizations or individuals operating on a part-time basis. The significance of these facets of the industry becomes apparent when shingle and shake export figures are compared to the value of shipments from the shingle mills. In 1973 export values were $80 million which exceeds mill shipment figures by $12 million. Canada's primary export market for shingles and shakes is the U.S.A. and modest quantities are also taken by the United Kingdom and West Germany.

Particle Board Plants . . .

pay $10 million in salaries and wages to 1200 workers,

ship $47 million worth of products.

Particle board manufacture, which

83
Pulpwood logging operations in eastern Canada

84
Loading lumber on the British Columbia coast. In 1974, lumber accounted for almost 23 per cent of Canada's forest products export income.

84

consists of bonding wood flakes, shavings, and other wood residues under heat and pressure with synthetic resin binders, is increasing in importance. The industry has developed largely since 1955 and, in 1973, 11 plants were in operation. A large portion of the particle board produced is absorbed by the domestic market.

All Secondary Wood Industries...
pay $229 million in salaries and wages to 39 200 workers,
ship $895 million worth of products,
export $68 million worth of products.

The Paper and Allied Industries...
pay $1.248 billion in salaries and wages to 123 200 workers,
ship $5.271 billion worth of products,
export $2.675 billion worth of products.
About 70 per cent of production by the paper and allied industries comes from the pulp and paper mills. The remaining production is made up by the output of a number of paper-converting industries.

Pulp and Paper Mills...
pay $884 million in salaries and wages to 80 100 workers,
ship $3.791 billion worth of products,
export $2.616 billion worth of products.

This industry covers pulp mills producing both chemical and mechanical pulp as well as paper mills and combined pulp and paper mills manufacturing newsprint, book and writing paper, kraft paper, paperboard, and building and insulating board. It has been for many years a leading element in the Canadian economy as a producer, employer, and exporter.

In 1973, 146 pulp and paper mills operated in Canada, and Quebec claimed the largest share of the output with 32 per cent of mill shipment values. She was followed by British Columbia with 26 per cent and Ontario with 25 per cent. For raw materials, the mills rely mainly on spruce, balsam fir, jack pine, and hemlock among the softwoods and the poplars among the hardwoods.

Canada is the world's second largest producer of pulp and the leading exporter. The U.S.A., despite her position as the world leader in pulp production, is Canada's pre-eminent customer for all types of pulp. Japan, the United Kingdom and West Germany, are also large buyers. Much of Canada's pulp for shipment is eventually converted both at home and abroad into an enormous range of paper and paperboard products. Some highly refined pulps, however, are shipped to the chemical industry in Can-

87
Particle boards vary in appearance depending upon the size of wood particles from which they are made. This board, made from relatively large flakes of aspen wood, is used extensively in the house-building trade.

87

85
Veneer ready for the drier in a British Columbia plywood plant

86

86
Shingles, both functional and decorative, are featured on many modern buildings.

85

ada and elsewhere for conversion into rayon, cellophane, photofilm, plastics, explosives and other products.

In both the production and export of newsprint, Canada is the world leader. By far the larger part of the newsprint produced is exported and the U.S.A. is again the major purchaser. The United Kingdom, Australia, Brazil, and Mexico are also important customers.

The diversity of production within the pulp and paper mills tends to be obscured by the importance attached to pulp and newsprint. It is noteworthy that in 1973 the mills shipped over 980 thousand tons (890 kt) of printing and writing papers, more than 660 thousand tons (600 kt) of wrapping and packaging papers, about 160 thousand tons (145 kt) of building papers, over 2 million tons (1800 kt) of paper board, plus building boards valued in excess of $76 million. There are also many by-products resulting from mill operations including such items as alcohol, vanillin, cement additives, road binders, turpentine, and tall oil. A large part of this wide range of products is absorbed by the domestic market.

Paper-Converting Plants...

pay $364 million in salaries and wages to 43 100 workers,

88
Aerial view of a Nova Scotian pulp and paper mill
89
This newsprint roll is just over 27 feet (8.2 m) in width and weighs about 10 tons (9 t). It is being slit into various widths to meet customer requirements.

88

ship $1.480 billion worth of products,

export $59 million worth of products.

The paper-converting industries of Canada further manufacture part of the primary output of the pulp and paper mills. They produce composition roofing and sheathing, consisting of paper felt saturated with asphalt or tar and sometimes coated with a mineral surfacing; paper boxes and bags; and a host of miscellaneous items such as waxed paper, envelopes, toilet paper, drinking cups, and paper towels. In contrast to the basic pulp and paper industry, the paper-converting industries market their products mainly within Canada.

Smaller Ventures of Interest . . .

Canada has two small industries somewhat out of the mainstream of commercial forestry yet contributing specialized products which have come to be associated particularly with the Canadian scene.

Christmas Trees

Although accurate figures are not available it is estimated that Canada produced about 5.3 million Christmas trees in 1973.

90

91

90
To protect Christmas trees from breakage and reduce the space occupied in transit, this machine wraps each tree in a plastic net stocking.

91
Happiness is early spring and maple taffy!

Exports in the same year amounted to 3.3 million trees valued at $4 million. The main export market is the U.S.A. with minor shipments going to a number of countries in and around the Caribbean.

Canada's major Christmas tree producing provinces are Nova Scotia, Quebec, British Columbia, Ontario, and New Brunswick. Balsam fir is the species most heavily harvested, but spruce, Douglas-fir, and plantation-grown Scots pine are also favoured trees.

Growers now face stiff competition from artificial Christmas trees and current emphasis is placed on producing better-quality natural trees and seeing that they reach the market in top condition. Many Christmas trees are sheared with special knives or hand clippers to encourage development of the dense, conical form that is in demand. Mechanized baling of individual trees, using twine or plastic net, is increasingly practised as a means of minimizing breakage in handling and saving space in transportation.

Maple Syrup

In eastern Canada the sugar maple tree is the basis of a unique forest food industry. When there is a combination of sunny days and frosty nights during early spring, the high-sugar-content sap of this tree flows freely. Holes are bored in the trunk and wooden spouts or metal spiles are inserted. Pails are hung on these projections to catch the dripping sap and from time to time they are emptied by an operator who makes his rounds by horse, tractor, truck, or, perhaps, snowmobile. In more modern operations, the tree taps are connected to plastic pipelines which feed by gravity, or in some cases by vacuum pump, to a central collecting point where boiling takes place.

About 30 to 40 gallons (135 to 185ℓ) must be boiled down to produce a gallon (4.5ℓ) of syrup and this represents about the average seasonal production of one tree. Factory products made from maple syrup include soft sugar, hard sugar, maple butter, and taffy.

Traditionally, maple syrup time is an occasion for partying and pancake festivals. In the time-honoured ritual of sugaring-off, thick, hot syrup is poured into containers of clean snow and the resulting taffy is wound on a stick and savoured by young and old alike.

Canada produced $13 million worth of maple syrup and maple sugar in 1974. In the same year, exports of these products earned $6.5 million mainly in the U.S.A. market.

The View Beyond the Trees

92

"Today I have grown taller from walking with the trees."

— James Russell Lowell

Man and the Forest

The forest is a vital, pulsing complex of living things, and at the centre of this complex is man himself. In Canada it was man who penetrated the forest and wrought the greatest changes. He removed countless trees for wood and fibre. He burned them accidentally, maliciously. He disrupted forest soils with highways, railroads, and logging roads. With the passage of time his demands on the forest have increased enormously.

Man first used the forest with the notion that it was inexhaustible and later with the thought that perhaps, in an unclearly perceived future, the forest harvest might just possibly reach a limit. And now, in recent times, he has realized with shattering clarity that he is fast approaching the point where even Canada's mighty forest resources may no longer be able to cope with his demands for more.

With this knowledge has come the further realization that the forest is a place of other values of consequence to his continued well-being. Forests are for wood certainly, but they are also for water, and for wildlife, and for solitude, and for the re-creation of human spirits.

Management is the key to maximum sustained harvests as well as to the variety of forest values we seek. It is based on detailed knowledge of forestry and the intricate ecological balances that obtain. It is, however, markedly influenced by man's individual, corporate, and collective goals. Man, the great adjuster of Nature, must come to terms with himself before he can hope to manipulate the forest ecosystem for his own greatest good.

Water and the Forest

In most parts of Canada water is available in copious supply but local shortages do occur. Sometimes, too, water quality is less than desirable and, of course, there are times when too much water creates problems.

Demand for water is expanding with increasing population and greater diversity of production. The quantities of water used are worthy of some consideration. In industry it takes 65 000 gallons (295 500 l) of water to produce a ton of steel, 365 000 gallons (1.7 Ml) for a ton of rayon yarn, and 300 gallons (1400l) for a barrel of beer. Food items are important. Enough wheat to make a 2½ pound (1 kg) loaf of bread requires 300 gallons (1400l) of water to grow. And then, of course, there is the everyday use of water in Canadian homes. This may

93

94
Most of the irrigation water impounded by southern Alberta's Waterton Dam comes from the mountains and foothills of the eastern Rockies in the background. Judicious forest management in these areas is vital to the future well-being of irrigated agriculture.

93

94

93
A wisely managed forest protects watersheds and exerts a beneficial influence on water quality and stream flow.

run anywhere from 75 to 150 gallons (340 to 680ℓ) per person per day.

Major parts of many river catchments in Canada lie within the forested landscape and changes in forest cover have a direct bearing on many aspects of water production and stream flow. Forest removal by logging or fire generally results in more water reaching stream channels over a shorter time. This, in turn, means a greater capacity to move sediment and debris which may originate from the cut or burned areas as well as from erosion of stream banks. It also means there is less opportunity for water to enter the groundwater storage reservoir.

The downstream effect of major changes in the headwater forest pattern can be far-reaching and at times devastating. Flooding is often a result, and, besides the more obvious damage which occurs, flood waters carrying additional sediment frequently lead to problems for domestic water supply, irrigation, and fish life.

95

To learn more about the water produced on this small, forested Ontario basin, stream flow is monitored using a v-notch weir and associated water-level recorder.

96

Measuring depth and water content of late-season snowpack on the Wilson Creek Experimental Watershed. This project, on the forested eastern slopes of Riding Mountain National Park in Manitoba, seeks answers to flooding and sedimentation problems which plague downstream agricultural lands.

A thorough assessment of a forested basin should indicate the relative importance of water and timber production. Conceivably, water supply might prove so important and a headwaters so vulnerable that any interference with forest cover would be unacceptable. On the other hand, perhaps selective logging might effect only minor changes in stream flow and cause little, if any, lowering of water quality while still permitting a valuable timber harvest.

There are, of course, other values besides timber and water which may influence management decisions. The need to manage all relevant values to realize the best combination of benefits has led to the concept of integrated resource management on a watershed basis. The concept, which is gaining increasing acceptance in Canada, recognizes the complex interactions which prevail within natural systems and the need for a better understanding of these processes.

As part of her contribution to UNESCO's International Hydrological Decade programme (1965-1974) Canada now operates more than 40 small catchment basins designed to yield a wide variety of information on the hydrology of watersheds. Among these are a number of projects, such as the Marmot Creek Experimental Basin on the east slopes of the Rocky Mountains in Alberta, where forest cover predominates and where information is gathered and assessed on many aspects of the forest in relation to stream flow and water quality.

In addition to acquiring basic information, Canada has also made a start on practical integrated resource management on a watershed basis. One of the earliest and most forestry-oriented projects was the joint federal-provincial Eastern Rockies Forest Conservation Board programme. This organization began operations in 1947 over a 9000-square-mile (23 000 km²) region of mountain peaks, forests, and grazing lands along the east slopes of the Rocky Mountains in Alberta. Within its area, the Board exercised control over logging operations, grazing, recreational activities, mineral exploration, and mining, primarily with a view to ensuring plentiful, good-quality water in the Saskatchewan River system which has major importance for all three prairie provinces. In 1973, with the termination of its mandate, this Board's responsibilities were assumed by the Government of Alberta.

Other noteworthy examples of practical integrated resource management are found in the 37 Conservation Authorities functioning in Ontario. These repre-

97
Countless lakes within Canada's forested landscape offer lively and rewarding action for angling enthusiasts.

98
Trail riders skirt the forested shores of Manitoba's Clear Lake.

sent groups of municipalities working together on a watershed basis and concerning themselves with the management of water, soil, forests, recreation, and wildlife.

In Manitoba too, one watershed conservation district embracing a number of rural municipalities is in operation and several more are in the planning stage.

Recreation and the Forest

Forest landscape plays an important role in the recreational pursuits of Canadians and visitors to Canada. It is difficult to conceive of our forested parks deprived of their cover. Trees are taken for granted in the natural pattern of things, yet without them the prospect is stark and unattractive.

Canada ranks fifth in importance in international tourism preceded by the U.S.A., Italy, Spain, and France. The total spent by international and domestic travellers amounts to more than $3.5 billion per annum. Statistics are too sketchy to permit other than a guess at the proportion of this considerable income which can be associated directly or indirectly with activities in the forested landscape. Nevertheless, it has been suggested that the figure is in the vicinity of $1 billion.

98

The demand for recreation in Canada is expanding rapidly and all indications suggest that it is not likely to slacken in the foreseeable future. Leisure time is increasing and population is growing and becoming increasingly urbanized. In 1971, 17 companies were identified as being on a four-day work week. A mere six months later this figure had increased to 60. It has also been estimated that by the year 2000 the total Canadian population will have some 350 billion hours of time at its disposal. It will spend about 5 per cent of this time working. Forty per cent will be spent in eating, sleeping and personal maintenance while the remaining 55 per cent will be free time. A further indicator of the pressures for recreation that can be anticipated is the forecast that population will rise by about 67 per cent by the year 2001 and that 94 per cent of the people will then be located in urban regions.

There are essentially four areas providing forest recreational opportunities in Canada. These are the forest tracts leased to woodland operators, national parks, provincial parks, and other areas of forest land.

Forests that have been open for logging have not always been available to recreationists; in fact, the early attitude was to keep the public out primarily on the grounds of vandalism, increased road costs, liability, fire, and safety. Over the years this situation has changed as the people have come to realize that the land in question is their land and woodland operators have recognized that this is indeed a fact of life and concessions are necessary. The forest industry has opened some 24 000 miles (39 000 km) of road to the public and some companies are providing camping sites, boat launching ramps, picnic grounds, and other amenities.

The national and provincial parks of Canada together occupy an area of 85 million acres (34.4 Mha) and play a major role in outdoor recreation. At present there are 28 national parks and one national park reserve in Canada. The one reserve along with 10 of the parks was added to the system between 1968 and 1972. This is a measure of the concern felt by Canadian society with respect to the need for more recreational areas. Some of the largest forested parks are from 2000 to 4000 square miles (5000 to 10 000 km²) in extent and are concentrated in the north and west. National park use is increasing. In 1965, 9.8 million people visited the system and by 1971 this figure had increased to 14 million.

The national parks policy as related to forest land is to maintain scenic and recreational values with a minimum disturbance of the natural features. Fellings for fire and erosion control and for the maintenance of forest health are kept to a minimum and commercial logging is not permitted. Public appreciation of the natural environment is fostered by the provision of exhibits, lectures, leaflets, and nature trails.

Canada has more than 1800 provincial parks covering some 96 000 square miles (249 000 km²) and many of the larger ones, ranging up to 7000 square miles (18 000 km²), are at least partly forested. Although the principal objective in these parks is to provide land for recreational use, certain sites are preserved for scientific purposes and commercial logging is permitted in some instances. In 1970, close to 42 million people visited the provincial parks.

Outside of the parks and areas devoted to logging there are still considerable tracts of forest land with excellent recreation potential. However, present access tends to limit the use of the more northern forests to the occasional angler, hunter, or canoeist while some otherwise attractive areas closer to population centres are currently lightly used because of the presence of biting insects.

100

99
Fun in the forest is by no means restricted to the summer months.
100,101
Wilderness camping and hiking — an adventure in the forest

99

101

Beaver dams help to keep streams
flowing in dry summer months.

Wildlife
and the Forest

Within Canada's forest landscape there is a wide variety of animal life while the rivers and lakes fed from forested watersheds support an abundance of fish. The forests, too, are rich in birds, both resident and migratory. This varied population of living creatures plays an important role in the lives of Canadians and in the experience of visitors to the Canadian scene. Animals, fish, and birds populate three major biomes, or living areas: the forest, the grasslands, and the tundra. By far the largest of these is the forest. The importance of wildlife can, in some cases, be established in economic terms, but there are also many intangible benefits to be considered.

In the 1973-74 fur season, almost 2.8 million pelts valued at $32.7 million were taken from the wild by Canadian trappers, many of them Indians and Eskimos. It has been estimated that there is also something in the order of 2 million hunters, both resident and non-resident, who operate in Canada. These people are concerned with bagging everything from big game to game birds. Their contribution to the country's economy,

104

103, 104
Forest wildlife on the move; a source of continuing appeal to people of all ages

105
Growing numbers of avid bird watchers will always find their powers of observation challenged within the forest. Colour, light, and shade combine to partially camouflage a red-tailed hawk.

105

106
The well-being of the moose and many other attractive species of forest wildlife is dependent upon man's wisdom when he manipulates the forest ecosystem.

coupled with the value of the wild fur trade, is probably in excess of $200 million per annum.

The return from fishing and angling is even more impressive. In 1973, Canada's inland fisheries produced 99 million pounds (45 kt) of fish valued at $19.4 million. The sports fishery now attracts approximately 3 million people from Canada and the United States who spend an estimated $500 million annually and it is believed that this figure may well reach the $1 billion mark by 1980.

An unknown but undoubtedly substantial amount is also added to the economy through the activities of photographers, bird-watchers, and nature lovers in general.

Of course, only part of the economic returns from wildlife is generated within the forest landscape. Furs are produced by seals as well as beaver; much sport fishing is done in coastal waters; and even the relatively treeless prairies attract their share of hunters and naturalists.

For many people, however, wildlife

holds values incapable of expression in monetary terms. The sight of salmon heading home to spawn, the bugling sounds of elk on autumn air, or the touch of a deer's muzzle may each contribute in a unique way to human recreation in the truest sense of that word.

The influence of wildlife on the forest, and forest management on wildlife, produces some interesting conflicts in terms of the values that man expects to derive from these resources. Deer and elk may damage trees by browsing, especially in plantation areas. Beavers are often responsible for flooding problems on forest roads and highways. Smaller rodents may adversely affect natural regeneration and girdle certain trees. Grouse sometimes cause damage in natural regeneration or plantations, and pine grosbeaks are noted for the problems they can create in removing buds especially in Scots pine Christmas tree plantations.

In addition to direct damage, there are some indirect problems associated with wildlife that have particular importance for commercial forest operators and forest resource management agencies. Unthinking hunters, anglers, and nature lovers, attracted by wildlife, can cause devastating damage by fire as well as

presenting needless hazards through careless handling of firearms and improper operation of high-powered cars.

On the other hand, the way in which a forest is managed may create problems for wildlife. Still fresh in memory are the adverse effects on birds and young Atlantic salmon of DDT sprayed over New Brunswick forests to control spruce budworm. Alterations of drainage or water flow patterns, road building, and disturbances by camping, walking, riding, snowmobiling, fire suppression, modern logging and so on, may all exert sometimes obvious, sometimes subtle effects on wildlife populations.

At the start of this section, mention was made of the important role of man in relation to the forest. Man-wrought alterations in the forest may quickly result in changes in the water cycle, in recreation potentials, and in wildlife population and habits. All these changes can, in turn, produce direct and indirect effects on man himself both for good and ill. For Canada's foresters and land managers the challenge of integrating the management of these resources is formidable indeed. It demands research, much patience, and great understanding of the ecology involved and particularly of man's own integral role in that ecology.

Forestry Education and the Profession of Forestry

Under the terms of the British North America Act, Canada's provinces are responsible for the organization and development of forestry education. For those seeking professional careers in forestry there are six university-based forestry schools. There are also opportunities for technical training provided through a number of regional colleges, community colleges, institutes, and provincial forest services.

Four university forestry schools located at the University of British Columbia, the University of Toronto, Laval University, and the University of New Brunswick were established more than 50 years ago. These schools were founded in response to public concern for forest conservation and for the proper protection and utilization of timber. In the 1960's, their interests broadened considerably to encompass all aspects of forest resource management and two additional schools were established in 1970 at Lakehead University and at the University of Alberta.

The goal of these schools is to help Canadians enjoy the maximum economic, environmental, and social advantage from the country's forests and forest lands by their interlocking activities in education, research, and community service. They produce professional forest resource managers, forest and wood scientists, forest engineers, and teachers of forestry.

The six forestry schools are not in competition with one another or, indeed, with the technical schools which are concerned with satisfying other areas of forestry education. To achieve their stated goals more effectively they are united in the Association of University Forestry Schools of Canada.

At the present time the schools are

107

107
This young lady and her sister students at Lakehead University and other forestry schools confirm that the profession of forestry is no longer an all-male preserve.

108
In the forest entomology laboratory at the University of New Brunswick, specimens are examined in the course of slide preparation.

108

vitally concerned with improving their capacities to respond to increasing demands for teaching, research, and advisory services. The far-ranging concepts of integrated resource management born of a rapidly growing public awareness of, and demand for, the diverse values to be derived from forest land have brought about a reassessment of traditional forestry education patterns. Growing and changing requirements in this area have emphasized the need for greater financial support for the schools from their parent universities, from provincial and federal governments, and from forest industries.

Technical training in forestry is available at a number of institutions across Canada as listed in the section, "A Directory of Canadian Forestry". Full diploma courses are available at many of these, but in some instances instruction is limited to one or two years and students must transfer to other schools to complete their training.

In both the areas of technical and professional education there is growing provision for training in fields allied to forestry such as forest products, wildlife biology, water resources, parks and recreation, and resources management in general. In some instances, courses on the above topics are available at undergraduate or graduate levels in the universities or schools which provide the forestry training programmes, while in other cases they are available at institutions having no direct involvement with basic forestry programmes.

Besides formal forestry education in the universities and technical training

109
Forestry students from the British Columbia Institute of Technology use a stick to help pass a diameter tape around the trunk of a massive western red cedar.

111
At Sir Sandford Fleming College of Applied Arts and Technology in Ontario, forest technology students make checks on tree seedling growth.

110
About 25 000 young people, both boys and girls, are members of conservation study groups sponsored by provincial forestry associations. Here, members of the Junior Forest Wardens of British Columbia learn something of a forester's tools of trade.

113

113
A core sample taken with an increment borer gives these forestry technicians information on the age and life history of a tree.

112
Traditionally, Canadian forestry has been associated with wildland and this embraces more than simply trees. In Newfoundland, professional foresters are studying peatlands and this work may lead to important economic developments for the province. Here, tourists in Newfoundland's Terra Nova National Park discard footwear to become acquainted with the peatlands.

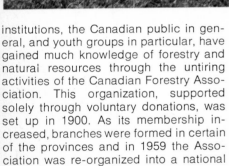

112

institutions, the Canadian public in general, and youth groups in particular, have gained much knowledge of forestry and natural resources through the untiring activities of the Canadian Forestry Association. This organization, supported solely through voluntary donations, was set up in 1900. As its membership increased, branches were formed in certain of the provinces and in 1959 the Association was re-organized into a national federation of provincial associations.

By its early efforts with the public and leaders of government, the Association prompted action which led to the establishment of Canada's first School of Forestry at the University of Toronto in 1907. As well as maintaining its interest in advanced forestry education the Association has also played a direct and important role in bringing forestry and natural resource matters to the attention of schoolchildren across the nation. Each year in the Prairie Provinces alone, approximately 200 000 students and 6000 teachers attend films and talks presented by staffs of the various associations.

Annually, the Canadian Forestry Association and its member associations sponsor National Forest Week in a vigorous attempt to concentrate public attention on the forest resource. All aspects of modern communications are utilized to emphasize the many-faceted benefits to be derived from the forest and the vital need for its protection and wise management. The cartoon character, Smokey Bear, carries the fire-hazard message far and wide, forestry poster competitions for youngsters burgeon, the concept of Arbor Day is promoted, and the virtues of conserving the forest heritage are extolled.

Films, brochures, and other publications on forestry and environmental matters are produced for the general public by various provincial resource authorities and by the Canadian Forestry Service in Ottawa. A prominent bestseller published by the Service is *Native Trees of Canada.* This authoritative work is available in both French and English editions. Another significant publication is *The Forestry Chronicle,* the bi-monthly professional and technical periodical published by the Canadian Institute of Forestry — Institut Forestier du Canada. Its objective is to improve the management and use of the Canadian forest land resource and encourage a wider understanding of forestry.

The Canadian Society of Forest Engineers, founded in 1908 under an Ontario provincial charter, was Canada's first national body of foresters. By 1950, the Society's membership had expanded from its original 12 members to 1127, and in the same year it was incorporated under a Dominion charter as the Canadian Institute of Forestry. It assumed its present dual designation Canadian Institue of Forestry — Institut Forestier du Canada in 1968 and in 1974 membership reached 2218. The Institute is a national organization of foresters, forest scientists, and affiliates. In addition to its present headquarters at Macdonald College, Ste. Anne de Bellevue, Quebec, it is represented across the country by a total of 22 sections which permits a close association with local forestry problems and objectives.

In British Columbia, Ontario, Quebec, and New Brunswick, provincial professional foresters' associations have been set up. By law in these provinces, certain documents pertaining to the management of Crown forests must be prepared and certified by individuals registered in these associations.

Canadian forestry technicians have sought to establish their identity through provincial organizations as well. By 1971, they had set up four associations of forest technicians and two societies of forest officers.

Forestry Research

The largest forestry research organization in Canada is the Canadian Forestry Service which operates within the Environmental Management Service of the Canada Department of the Environment. The objective of this Service is to promote the preservation, enhancement, and wise use of a healthy, attractive, and bountiful forest resource and terrestrial environment for the economic and social benefit of all Canadians.

The Service is concerned with providing information useful in the formulation of improved government and private policies, programmes, and plans bearing on the forestry sector. Its main research and development activities are related to the production of wood at competitive costs and the growing and maintenance of trees and forests where the primary values are social and environmental in nature. Besides these more applied aspects of research, the Service also undertakes fundamental research in such areas as plant physiology, taxonomy, and wood properties to gather information of current or potential importance to the overall programme.

114

114
A trussed rafter undergoes tests to determine snow load capacity at the Eastern Forest Products Laboratory of the Canadian Forestry Service.

115
A white elm is given root injection treatment with a newly developed chemical (CFS 1020) for the control of Dutch elm disease. This approach has shown promise of stopping spread of the disease in valuable individual elm shade trees.

115

116
By applying intricate culturing techniques to tissue taken from living trees,
federal scientists have grown new
plantlets. This non-sexual reproduc-
tion process, know as cloning, produced the white spruce shown in the
flask. Successfully developed, the
cloning system could vastly improve
regeneration programmes by speed-
ing production of large quantities of
guaranteed, high-quality planting stock
originating from selected superior
parent trees.

116

Aside from its predominant research
function, the Service has an operational
role with respect to continuing its coun-
try-wide Forest Insect and Disease Survey, providing forestry input to environmental impact studies such as those
being conducted for the James Bay
development and the Mackenzie Valley
pipeline, and servicing the forestry needs
of other federal departments.

Through its extension services the
Canadian Forestry Service brings relevant forestry information to resource
managers and the general public. It also
maintains effective communications on
international forestry matters with a wide
range of organizations including the
International Union of Forestry Research
Organizations, the Timber Committee of
the Economic Commission for Europe,
several subsidiary bodies of the Food
and Agriculture Organization of the
United Nations, and the Organization for
Economic Co-operation and Development. Assistance and advice on forestry
are provided for the Canadian International Development Agency which is
responsible for administering Canada's
foreign aid programme, and tours and
visits of foreign forestry representatives
are also arranged.

The Canadian Forestry Service has a
headquarters establishment, six regional

research centres, two forest products
laboratories, and five research institutes.
With the exception of the headquarters,
each of the above components is
attached to one of five regions of the
Environmental Management Service and
its work is closely co-ordinated at this
regional level with that of the balance of
the units within the Environmental Management Service which are concerned
with wildlife, water, and land. This ar-
rangement provides the basis for a unique
multi-disciplinary team approach to environmental problems clearing the way
towards a better realization of the concept of integrated resource management.

Recent research of interest conducted
by the Service includes studies on clear-
cutting, fire, road building, and the use
of herbicides, pesticides, and fertilizers,
all with respect to impact on the forest
environment. A new systemic fungicide
has also been developed which shows
promise for arresting the growth of the
fungus which causes Dutch elm disease.
In the light of prevalent petro-chemical-
based adhesive shortages a significant
advance for the wood products industry
has been the patenting of a new water-
proof adhesive made from waste sulphite
pulping liquor. Remote sensing and
inventory research has been concerned
with operational trials of large-scale

aerial photography and a detailed appraisal of imagery produced by the Earth
Resources Technology Satellite.

Besides its own in-house research
commitments, the Canadian Forestry
Service also has additional work carried
out by contract as well as through the
Department of the Environment science
subvention programme. The latter provides support for non-government scientists in developing their own research
proposals in areas of interest common
to both parties. To help finance research
directed specifically towards the reduction of water pollution caused by pulp
and paper operations, the federal government also set up an initial $5.5 million
fund for the 1970-76 period. This will be
followed by an annual funding of $1.5
million for a further five years.

Certain of Canada's provinces maintain a forestry research capacity within
appropriate provincial government departments. Prominent in this area are
British Columbia, Ontario, and Quebec.
Most of the other provinces are concerned with development projects from
time to time and some have limited
research programmes. In certain cases,
provincial personnel engage in co-oper-
ative projects with the Canadian Forestry
Service, and provincial and federal representatives also serve on a number of

117
Within Canada's boreal forests there are large tracts of muskeg supporting commercial stands of timber. The Forest Management Institute of the Canadian Forestry Service is conducting considerable research with this air cushion test vehicle to find a way of transporting logging equipment and logs over soft terrain during the open season.

118
A researcher from the Forest Research Branch of the Ontario Ministry of Natural Resources carefully excavates and studies the rooting system of a white pine.

119
Located near Chalk River, Ontario, the 38-square-mile (98 km²) Petawawa Forest Experiment Station is one of the oldest forest research establishments in Canada. Silvicultural research commenced here in 1918.

120
The modern laboratories of the Pulp and Paper Research Institute of Canada, located at Pointe Claire in the Province of Quebec

121
Sitka spruce growing in styromoulds as part of a provenance testing programme at the research greenhouse of the Cowichan Lake Experimental Station in British Columbia

121

advisory or research planning bodies across the country. Part of the function of these groups is to ensure effective co-ordination of federal and provincial forestry research programmes.

To service the research needs of her pulp and paper industry, Canada has relied heavily on the work of the Pulp and Paper Research Institute of Canada located at Pointe Claire, Quebec. The Institute conducts a basic programme of research which is of broad interest to the industry. This work is financed largely by assessments on the 56 member companies which represent the industry across the country. Contract research is also conducted by the Institute on a cost-reimbursement basis for companies, or groups of companies, in pulp and paper and allied fields. In addition, technical information is provided to the pulp and paper industry and in some instances to other industries and the general public. The Institute, in co-operation with McGill University, has a number of graduate students working towards advanced degrees on projects connected with pulp and paper technology.

In 1975, the Forest Engineering Research Institute of Canada — Institut Canadien de Recherches en Genie Forestier was incorporated to carry out research and development work in the areas of harvesting, transportation, and use of wood. The Institute was designed to bring together elements of logging research activity located within the Canadian Forestry Service and the Pulp and Paper Research Institute of Canada. Its operations are jointly financed by the federal government and forest industry companies.

While many of Canada's universities undertake research projects which may eventually be utilized by the forestry sector, it is those with established forestry schools that make the major contributions. Forestry research is concentrated most strongly at the forestry schools attached to the University of British Columbia, the University of Toronto, Laval University, and the University of New Brunswick. Given the required human and material resources, forestry research can be expected to expand at both the University of Alberta and Lakehead University. Research at the forestry schools has been supported for many years by various federal grant programmes sponsored by the Department of the Environment, its predecessor departments, and the National Research Council of Canada (a Crown corporation). Further finances come from such sources as provincial government agencies, the universities concerned, and forest industries.

Besides its support of various aspects of forestry research through grants, the National Research Council of Canada also conducts some in-house forestry studies. At the provincial level, too, there are eight research councils or foundations. Of these establishments, the ones located in British Columbia and Ontario have been most directly concerned with research in the forest products and forest resource areas. These provincial organizations are financed almost wholly by a combination of provincial government grants and contract income.

Although forest industry was engaged in some aspects of research as early as 1913, it was not until after 1950 that any substantial expansion of these activities took place. Early work was primarily concerned with silviculture and allied areas of study, but there is now a substantial capability in forest products research and most of the pulp and paper companies maintain laboratories for research relative to their own particular products. Some companies are also developing logging equipment and improving logging methods to cope better with their specific operating problems.

A Directory of Canadian Forestry

This section is intended as a general guide to governmental agencies, educational institutions, professional associations, etc., which relate to forestry in Canada.

Provincial Government Agencies

The following agencies may be contacted for information on provincial forest policy and administration, the management of the provincial forest resource, and on existing provincial forest research programmes.

Newfoundland

Newfoundland Forest Service,
Department of Forestry and Agriculture,
Building 180,
Pleasantville,
St. John's, Newfoundland A1A 1P9

Prince Edward Island

Forestry Branch,
Department of Agriculture and Forestry,
Box 2000,
Charlottetown, Prince Edward Island
C1A 7N8

Nova Scotia

Department of Lands and Forests,
1740 Granville Street,
Box 698,
Halifax, Nova Scotia B3J 2T9

New Brunswick

Forests Branch,
Department of Natural Resources,
Centennial Building,
Fredericton, New Brunswick E3B 5H1

Quebec

Direction générale des Forêts
Ministère des Terres et Forêts
200B, chemin Sainte-Foy
Québec (Québec) G1A 1P4

Ontario

Division of Forests,
Ministry of Natural Resources,
Whitney Block,
Parliament Buildings,
Toronto, Ontario M7A 1W3

Manitoba

Forestry Programs,
Operational Policy Division,
Department of Mines, Resources and
Environmental Management,
989 Century Street,
Winnipeg, Manitoba R3H 0W4

Saskatchewan

Forestry Branch,
Department of Tourism and
Renewable Resources,
Provincial Office Building,
Prince Albert, Saskatchewan S6V 1B5

Alberta

Alberta Forest Service,
Department of Energy and
Natural Resources,
Natural Resources Building,
Edmonton, Alberta T5K 1H4

British Columbia

British Columbia Forest Service,
Department of Lands, Forests,
and Water Resources,
Legislative Buildings,
Victoria, British Columbia V8V 1X5

Federal Government Departments and Agencies

Canadian Forestry Service,
Environmental Management Service,
Department of the Environment,
Ottawa, Ontario K1A 0H3
(For general information on Canadian forestry and forest research)

Newfoundland Forest Research Centre,
Canadian Forestry Service,
Bldg. 304, Pleasantville, P.O. Box 6028,
St. John's, Newfoundland A1C 5X8
(For federal forest research information pertaining to Newfoundland)

Maritimes Forest Research Centre,
Canadian Forestry Service,
P.O. Box 4000, College Hill,
Fredericton, New Brunswick E3B 5G4
(For federal forest research information pertaining to New Brunswick, Nova Scotia, and Prince Edward Island)

Laurentian Forest Research Centre,
Canadian Forestry Service,
1080 Route du Vallon, P.O. Box 3800,
Ste-Foy, Quebec G1V 4C7
(For federal forest research information pertaining to Quebec)

Great Lakes Forest Research Centre,
Canadian Forestry Service,
P.O. Box 490, 1219 Queen Street East,
Sault Ste. Marie, Ontario P6A 5M7
(For federal forest research information pertaining to Ontario)

Northern Forest Research Centre,
Canadian Forestry Service,
5320 - 122 Street,
Edmonton, Alberta T6H 3S5
(For federal forest research information pertaining to Alberta, Saskatchewan, Manitoba, the Yukon and Northwest Territories)

Pacific Forest Research Centre,
Canadian Forestry Service,
506 West Burnside Road,
Victoria, British Columbia V8Z 1M5

(For federal forest research information pertaining to British Columbia)

Chemical Control Research Institute,
Canadian Forestry Service,
25 Pickering Place,
Ottawa, Ontario K1A 0W3
(For federal research information on forest pest control)

Forest Fire Research Institute,
Canadian Forestry Service,
Nicol Building,
Ottawa, Ontario K1A 0W2
(For federal research information on forest fire)

Forest Management Institute,
Canadian Forestry Service,
Majestic Building,
Ottawa, Ontario K1A 0W2
(For federal research information on forest appraisal, forest productivity, logging, urban forestry, and remote sensing — also for information on metric conversion relative to forestry)

Insect Pathology Research Institute,
Canada Forestry Service,
P.O. Box 490, 1219 Queen Street East,
Sault Ste. Marie, Ontario P6A 5M7
(For federal research information on insect pathology)

Eastern Forest Products Laboratory,
Canadian Forestry Service,
Montreal Road,
Ottawa, Ontario K1A 0W5
(For federal research information on forest products east of the Manitoba-Ontario boundary)

Western Forest Products Laboratory,
Canadian Forestry Service,
6620 N.W. Marine Drive,
Vancouver, British Columbia V6T 1X2
(For federal research information on forest products west of the Manitoba-Ontario boundary)

Petawawa Forest Experiment Station,
Canadian Forestry Service,
Chalk River, Ontario K0J 1J0
(For federal research information on silviculture, tree genetics and improvement, tree seed, and forest fire)

Lands Directorate,
Environmental Management Service,
Department of the Environment,
Ottawa, Ontario K1A 0H3
(For information on the Canada Land Inventory)

Canadian Wildlife Service,
Environmental Management Service,
Department of the Environment,
Ottawa, Ontario K1A 0H3
(For information on Canadian wildlife)

Inland Waters Directorate,
Environmental Management Service,
Department of the Environment,

Ottawa, Ontario K1A 0H3
(For information on Canadian water resources)

Forest Products Group,
Resource Industries and
Construction Branch,
Department of Industry,
Trade and Commerce,
112 Kent Street,
Ottawa, Ontario K1A 0H5
(For information on trade and marketing of forest products)

National Parks Branch,
Department of Indian and
Northern Affairs,
400 Laurier Avenue West,
Ottawa, Ontario K1A 0H4
(For information on management of forests within the national parks)

Northern Natural Resources and
Environment Branch,
Department of Indian and
Northern Affairs,
400 Laurier Avenue West,
Ottawa, Ontario K1A 0H4
(For information on management of forests in the Yukon and Northwest Territories)

Department of Regional Economic
Expansion,
161 Laurier Avenue West,
Ottawa, Ontario K1A 0M4
(For information on regional forestry improvement programmes)

Forestry Education Institutions

Universities

Faculty of Forestry,
University of New Brunswick,
Fredericton, New Brunswick E3B 5A3

Faculté de foresterie et de géodésie
Université Laval
Cité universitaire,
Québec (Québec) G1K 7P4

Faculty of Forestry,
University of Toronto,
Toronto, Ontario M3J 1P3

School of Forestry,
Lakehead University,
Thunder Bay, Ontario P7B 5E1

Faculty of Forestry,
University of Alberta,
Edmonton, Alberta T6G 2E1

Faculty of Forestry,
University of British Columbia,
Vancouver, British Columbia V6T 1W5

Schools and Colleges offering Technical Training in Forestry

College of Trades and Technology,
P.O. Box 1693,
St. John's, Newfoundland A1C 5P7

Maritime Forest Ranger School,
Fredericton, New Brunswick E3B 4X6

Collège d'Enseignement général et
professionnel de Sainte-Foy
2410, chemin Sainte-Foy
Québec (Québec) G1V 1T3

Collège d'Enseignement général et
professionnel de Chicoutimi
543 est, rue Jacques-Cartier, C.P. 1148
Chicoutimi (Québec) G7H 5G4

Collège d'Enseignement général et
professionnel de Rimouski
60 ouest, rue de l'Évêché
Rimouski (Québec) G5L 4H6

Collège d'Enseignement général et
professionnel de la Gaspésie
C.P. 590
Gaspé (Québec) G0C 1R0

Collège d'Enseignement général et
professionnel John Abbott
C.P. 2000
Ste-Anne-de-Bellevue (Québec) H9X 3L9

Collège d'Enseignement général et
professionnel de Rouyn-Noranda
C.P. 1500, Rouyn
Cté de Rouyn-Noranda (Québec)
J9X 5E2

Collège d'Enseignement général et
professionnel de la Côte-Nord
(Campus Manicouagan)
537, boulevard Blanche
Hauterive (Québec) G5C 2B2

Service de l'éducation des adultes
Centre de foresterie
Duchesnay, Cté Portneuf
(Québec) G0A 3M0

Sir Sandford Fleming College,
Lindsay Campus,
33 Russell Street East,
Lindsay, Ontario K9V 2A2

Sault College of Applied Arts
and Technology,
P.O. Box 60,
Sault Ste. Marie, Ontario P6A 5L3

Algonquin College of Applied Arts
and Technology,
Upper Ottawa Valley Campus,
Pembroke, Ontario K8A 3K2

Lakehead University,
Thunder Bay, Ontario P7B 5E1

Kelsey Institute of Applied Arts
and Sciences,
P.O. Box 1520,
Saskatoon, Saskatchewan S7K 3R5

Northern Alberta Institute of Technology,
11762 - 106 Street,
Edmonton, Alberta T5G 2R1

Forest Technology School,

Northern Alberta Institute of Technology,
P.O. Box 880,
Hinton, Alberta T0E 1B0

British Columbia Institute of Technology,
3700 Willingdon Avenue,
Burnaby, British Columbia V5G 3H2

Malaspina College,
375 Kennedy Street,
Nanaimo, British Columbia V9R 2J3

Selkirk College,
P.O. Box 1200,
Castlegar, British Columbia V1N 3J1

College of New Caledonia,
2001 Central Street,
Prince George, British Columbia
V2N 1P8

Research Councils, Foundations, etc.

Nova Scotia Research Foundation,
P.O. Box 790,
Dartmouth, Nova Scotia B2Y 3Z7

New Brunswick Research and
Productivity Council,
College Hill Road,
Fredericton, New Brunswick

Forest Research Foundation,
Laval University,
Cité universitaire,
Quebec, Quebec G1P 7P4

Pulp and Paper Research Institute
of Canada
570 St. John's Boulevard,
Pointe Claire, Quebec H9R 3J9

Forest Products Research Society,
Eastern Canadian Section,
c/o Faculty of Forestry,
University of Toronto,
Toronto, Ontario M3J 1P3

Ontario Research Foundation,
Sheridan Park,
Mississauga, Ontario L5K 1B3

Manitoba Research Council,
401 York Road,
Winnipeg, Manitoba R3C 0P8

Saskatchewan Research Council,
University Campus,
Saskatoon, Saskatchewan S7N 0X1

Research Council of Alberta,
11315 - 87 Avenue,
Edmonton, Alberta T6G 2C2

British Columbia Research Council,
University of British Columbia,
Vancouver, British Columbia V6T 1W5

Foresters' Organizations

Canadian Institute of Forestry —
Institut Forestier du Canada,
Box 5000,

Macdonald College,
Ste. Anne de Bellevue, Quebec H0A 1C0

Association of Registered Professional
Foresters of New Brunswick,
Box 23,
Fredericton, New Brunswick E3B 4Y2

Corporation professionnelle des
ingénieurs forestiers du Québec
1415, chemin Sainte-Foy,
Québec (Québec) G1S 2N7

Ontario Professional Foresters'
Association,
Suite 34,
10235 Yonge Street,
Richmond Hill, Ontario

Association of British Columbia
Professional Foresters,
407 - 837 West Hastings Street,
Vancouver, British Columbia V6C 1B6

Forest Industry and Forest Products Associations

Nova Scotia Forest Products Association,
30 Mill Street,
Truro, Nova Scotia B2N 4A1

New Brunswick Forest Products
Association,
P.O. Box 1224,
Fredericton, New Brunswick E3B 5C8

Quebec Forest Industries Association,
Suite 508,
500 Grande Allée East,
Quebec, Quebec G1R 2J4

Canadian Pulp and Paper Association,
2300 Sun Life Building,
Montreal, Quebec H3B 2X9

Canadian Wood Council,
701 - 170 Laurier Avenue West,
Ottawa, Ontario K1P 5V5

Canadian Lumbermen's Association,
27 Goulburn Avenue,
Ottawa, Ontario K1N 8C7

Canadian Institute of Timber
Construction,
200 Cooper Street,
Ottawa, Ontario K2P 0G1

Ontario Forest Industries Association,
159 Bay Street,
Toronto, Ontario M5J 1J7

Manitoba Forest Products Association,
14G - 1975 Corydon Avenue,
Winnipeg, Manitoba R3P 0R1

Alberta Forest Products Association,
10428 - 123 Street,
Edmonton, Alberta T5M 0G2

Council of Forest Industries of
British Columbia,
1500 - 1055 West Hastings Street,
Vancouver, British Columbia V6E 2H1

Forestry Associations

Canadian Forestry Association,
185 Somerset Street West,
Ottawa, Ontario K2P 0J2

Newfoundland Forest Protection
Association,
Pleasantville,
Building 810,
St. John's, Newfoundland A1A 1P9

Nova Scotia Forestry Association,
6070 Quinpool Road,
Halifax, Nova Scotia B3L 1A1

Canadian Forestry Association of
New Brunswick,
Maritime Forest Ranger School Campus,
RR 5,
Fredericton, New Brunswick E3B 4X6

Association forestière québécoise, inc.
915 ouest, rue St-Cyrille
Québec (Québec) G1S 1T8

Ontario Forestry Association,
Room 209,
150 Consumers Road,
Willowdale, Ontario M2J 1P9

Manitoba Forestry Association,
Suite 2,
720 Dorchester Avenue,
Winnipeg, Manitoba R3M 0R5

Saskatchewan Forestry Association,
308 Poplar Crescent,
Saskatoon, Saskatchewan S7M 0A6

Alberta Forestry Association,
218 Alberta Block,
10526 Jasper Avenue,
Edmonton, Alberta T5J 1Z7

Canadian Forestry Association of
British Columbia,
Suite 410,
1200 West Pender Street,
Vancouver, British Columbia V6E 2S9

Selected References

Canada
Hosie, R. C. *Native Trees of Canada*
Queen's Printer for Canada, Ottawa, 1969
Price: Paper-bound $6.00 in Canada,
$7.20 outside Canada
Cat. No. Fo45-1969.1
Cloth-bound $9.50 in Canada,
$11.40 outside Canada
Cat. No. Fo45-1969.2

Rowe, J. S. *Forest Regions of Canada*
Information Canada, Ottawa, 1972
Price: $2.50 Cat. No. Fo47-1300

Potvin, Albert, *A Panorama of Canadian
Forests*
Information Canada, Ottawa, 1975
Price: $13.50 in Canada, $16.20 outside
Canada
Cat. No. Fo25-17/1975
(All available from Information Canada
bookshops at
1683 Barrington Street, Halifax,
Nova Scotia B3J 1Z9,
640 St. Catherine Street West, Montreal,
Quebec H3B 1B8,
171 Slater Street, Ottawa, Ontario K1A 0S9
221 Yonge Street, Toronto, Ontario
M5B 1N4,
393 Portage Avenue, Winnipeg,
Manitoba R3B 2C6,
800 Granville Street, Vancouver,
British Columbia V6Z 1K4,
and also from Canadian booksellers. These
publications are also available in French.)

The Forestry Chronicle
Canadian Institute of Forestry — Institut
Forestier du Canada, Bi-monthly.
Price: $10 per year in Canada, $12 per year
in other countries.
$2.50 for single copies.
(Available from Canadian Institute of Forestr
Box 5000, Macdonald College, Quebec
H0A 1C0)

Newfoundland
Page, Graham; Wilton, W. C.; and Thomas,
Tony. *Forestry in Newfoundland*
Newfoundland Forest Research Centre,
St. John's, 1974
Price: Free
(Available from Newfoundland Forest
Research Centre, Canadian Forestry Servic
P.O. Box 6028, St. John's, Newfoundland
A1C 5X8)

Prince Edward Island
Gaudet, J. F. *Native Trees and Woodland
Shrubs of Prince Edward Island*
Prince Edward Island Department of Agricu
ture and Forestry, Charlottetown, 1973
Price: Free
(Available from Forestry Branch, Departme
of Agriculture and Forestry, P.O. Box 2000,
Charlottetown, Prince Edward Island
C1A 7N8)

Nova Scotia
Saunders, Gary L. *Trees of Nova Scotia —
A Guide to Native and Exotic Species*
Nova Scotia Department of Lands and

Forests, Halifax, 1970
Price: $0.75
(Available from Nova Scotia Government
Bookstore, 1683 Barrington Street,
Halifax, Nova Scotia B3J 1Z9)

Saunders, Gary L. *The Man Who Couldn't
Stop Sneezing — A Fable About Wood*
Nova Scotia Department of Lands and
Forests, Halifax, 1969
Price: Single copies free
(Available from Nova Scotia Department
of Lands and Forests, Forest Resources
Education, P.O. Box 68, Truro, Nova Scotia
B2N 5B8)

New Brunswick
Anon. *Highlights — Calendar Year 1973*
New Brunswick Department of Natural
Resources, Fredericton, 1974
Price: Free

Tweeddale, R. E. (Executive Director).
Report of the Forest Resources Study 1974
Government of New Brunswick, New
Brunswick Forest Resources Study,
Fredericton, 1974
Price: $5.00
(Both available from Forests Branch,
New Brunswick Department of Natural
Resources, Centennial Building, Fredericton,
New Brunswick E3B 5H1)

Quebec
Anon. *Petite flore forestière du Québec*
Ministère des Terres et Forêts du Québec,
Québec, 1974
Price: $3.75
(Available from Editeur officiel du Québec,
2, rue St-Jean, Québec (Québec) G1R 1P8)

Anon. *Comment assurer le succès d'une
plantation*
Ministère des Terres et Forêts du Québec,
Québec
Price: Free

Anon. *La forêt du Québec*
Ministère des Terres et Forêts du Québec,
Québec, 1974
Price: Free
(Both available from Ministère des Terres et
Forêts,
200B, chemin Sainte-Foy, Québec (Québec)
G1A 1P4)

Ontario
Lambert, Richard S. with Pross, Paul.
Renewing Nature's Wealth
Ontario Department of Lands and Forests,
Toronto, 1967
Price: $9.50

Dixon, R. M. *The Forest Resources of Ontario*
Ontario Department of Lands and Forests,
Toronto, 1963
Price: $0.75
(Both available from Information Branch,
Ontario Ministry of Natural Resources,
Parliament Buildings, Toronto, Ontario
M7A 1W3
Note: Orders must be accompanied by remit-
tance payable to the Treasurer of Ontario.)

Manitoba
Cunningham, Harry A. *Just a Bunch of Trees*
Manitoba Department of Mines, Resources
and Environmental Management, Winnipeg,
1975
Price: Free
(Available from Extension Services, Opera-
tional Policy Division, Department of Mines,
Resources and Environmental Management
Box 9 - 989 Century Street, Winnipeg,
Manitoba R3H 0W4)

Calvert, R. C. *Tree Improvement in
Manitoba — Information Series No. 2*
Manitoba Department of Mines, Resources
and Environmental Management, Winnipeg,
1974
Price: Free
(Available from Department of Mines,
Resources and Environmental Management,
Box 7 - Building 2, 139 Tuxedo Boulevard,
Winnipeg, Manitoba R3N 0H6)

Saskatchewan
Newman, Duncan M. *Saskatchewan's Forest
Resources*
Saskatchewan Department of Tourism and
Renewable Resources, Regina, 1974
Price: Free

Anon. *Forest Conservation — Saskatchewan*
Saskatchewan Department of Natural
Resources, Regina
Price: Free
(Both available from Forestry Branch,
Saskatchewan Department of Tourism and
Renewable Resources, Provincial Office
Building, Prince Albert, Saskatchewan
S6V 1B5)

Alberta
The Conservation and Utilization Committee,
Task Force on the East Slopes Hearings.
*The Resources of the Foothills:
A Choice of Land Use Alternatives*
Alberta Department of Lands and Forests,
Alberta Department of the Environment,
Edmonton, 1973
Price: Free

Anon. *Alberta Forests*
Alberta Department of Lands and Forests,
Edmonton, 1974
Price: Free
(Both available from Alberta Forest Service,
Department of Energy and Natural Resources,
Natural Resources Building, Edmonton,
Alberta T5K 1H4)

British Columbia
Anon. *Management of British Columbia's
Forest Lands*
British Columbia Forest Service, Victoria, 1972
Price: Free

Anon. *Sustained Yield from British Columbia's
Forest Lands*
British Columbia Forest Service, Victoria,
1972
Price: Free
(Both distributed within Canada only. Contact
Information Division, British Columbia Forest
Service, Legislative Buildings, Victoria,
British Columbia V8V 1X5)

ForesTalk
British Columbia Forest Service, Victoria,
Quarterly
Price: Free
(Available from Information Division, British
Columbia Forest Service, Legislative
Buildings, Victoria, British Columbia V8V 1X5)

Northern Canada
Naysmith, John K. *The Future Value of
Canada's Northern Forests*
Department of Indian Affairs and Northern
Development, Ottawa, 1970
Price: Free. Cat. No R22-1/71-1

Naysmith, John K. *North of 60. Towards a
Northern Balance*
Department of Indian and Northern Affairs,
Ottawa, 1973
Price: Free. IAND Pub. No. QS-1501-000-
EE-A1

Anon. *North of 60. The Forests of Northern
Canada*
Department of Indian and Northern Affairs,
Ottawa, 1973
Price: Free. IAND Pub. No. QS-0849-000-
BB-A2
(All available from Department of Indian and
Northern Affairs, 400 Laurier Avenue West,
Ottawa, Ontario K1A 0H4. These publications
are also available in French.)

Metric Symbols

cm	=	centimetre
ha	=	hectare
kg	=	kilogram
km	=	kilometre
km²	=	square kilometre
kPa	=	kilopascal = 1 thousand pascals
kt	=	kilotonne = 1 thousand tonnes
l	=	litre
Mha	=	megahectare = 1 million hectares
M*l*	=	megalitre = 1 million litres
m	=	metre
m³	=	cubic metre
t	=	tonne = 1000 kilograms

Photography